Advance Praise for *Communicate That!*

If you are in the sales or marketing business and you are looking to increase your financial success, make *Communicate That!* part of your toolbox. Repetitive inclusion of Roshini's I-A-P™ method into each and every presentation will lead to bigger orders and better revenue production, regardless of the product, good, or service.

—**Mick Anselmo,** Sr. Vice President/Market Manager,
CBS Radio Minneapolis

Roshini's presentation training mechanisms really engaged me and my staff to become stronger communicators and deliver our intended messages. Her tools and techniques were easy to implement and helped us all think more strategically about our presentation opportunities. I've witnessed the improvement personally as well as across my team. I'd recommend this book to anyone looking to build confidence and clarity.

—**Jack Larson,** Vice President/General Manager,
Xcel Energy Center

As a novice children's book author, I was suddenly scheduled for several TV interviews. With the valued assistance of Roshini and following her I-A-P™ Formula, I was able to meet this challenge with much success, for which I am very grateful.

—**Marcella Barrett,** Author of *And The Tree Cried Out,*
Barrett Publishing, Dayton, OH

Roshini, you do have a gift for simple, elegant communication!

—**Nancy Maxfield Wilson,** Technical Consulting and Training,
NMW Consulting

COMMUNICATE THAT!

Your Toolbox for Powerful Presentations

Roshini Rajkumar
A Roshini Multi Media Production

Andover, Minnesota

ISBN 13: 978-0-9825912-2-2

Library of Congress Catalog Number: 2010922737

Printed in the United States of America
First Printing: March 2010

13 12 11 10 5 4 3 2 1

Andover, Minnesota

Expert Publishing, Inc.
14314 Thrush Street NW,
Andover, MN 55304-3330
1-877-755-4966
www.expertpublishinginc.com

To my brother, Roshan, who always amazes with his innate charisma, giving heart, and enchanting spirit. His natural WOW! inspires me more than he could ever know or words could adequately describe.

My love and respect always.

CONTENTS

ACKNOWLEDGMENTS

To my editor, Sharron Stockhausen, for her writing and book industry mentoring and instruction that started long before one word was written or typed.

To my book mentors Connie Anderson and Marly Cornell for their sound advice, trusted referrals, and enthusiasm to help me publish a WOW!

To all the clients who entrust me with teaching them how to use the I-A-P™ Formula to get to their WOW!'s. A special thanks to Kathy Wetzel at Great Clips Inc., Jack Larson and Kathy O'Connor at Xcel Energy Center, Jeff Holds at Phoenix Technology Solutions, Rick Morgan at Bowman and Brooke, Frederic Estes at Estes Gifts & News, and Barbara Brown at Meagher & Geer.

To audiences who experienced the I-A-P™ Formula before it came into book form, especially those at St. Catherine University, the University of Minnesota, The Woman's Club of Minneapolis, the St. Paul Chamber of Commerce, the Minneapolis Regional Chamber of Commerce, and the Edina Chamber of Commerce.

To dear friends and friendly enthusiasts who gave me encouragement to stay focused on my entrepreneurial path, especially Sharon Katz in Boston, Janie Peterson in Minneapolis, John Pompeo in Detroit, Laura Iavicoli in New York, Susan Snyder in Minneapolis, Michelle MacDonald in West St. Paul, Brenda Kroening in Burnsville, my banker Nancy Moschogianis in Edina, my accountant Scott Stone in Nashville, Mary Angela Baker in St. Paul, and Grant Harrell in Dallas.

To my trusted media buddies who didn't call me crazy when I left TV news to start my own business and picked up several meal and bar tabs when I launched, especially Joe Fryer in Minneapolis, Ken Stone in St. Paul, Neil Heinen in Madison, Jamie Strait in New York, Bryan

Karrick in Des Moines, and Charley Johnson in Fargo.

To my pre-readers for their enthusiasm and honest feedback: Molly Vlk in Phoenix, Barb Lee in Edina, and Scott Murray in Minneapolis.

To my voice coach, Larry Russo, for both his dedication to all things voice box and his inspiration, which empower me to explore and grow my own vocal capabilities.

To my parents, Concy Rajkumar and John Knoll, whose gift of unconditional love empowers me in ways that continually surprise me.

To my late father, Raj, for passionately living every day of his forty years, his lessons in cinematography, and for being the first to inspire me to WOW!

My warm thoughts and gratitude to the Minneapolis/St. Paul-area coffee shops where much of this book was written. In particular, Bread & Chocolate, Lucia's To Go, Namaste, YUM, and the Starbucks in Edina, St. Louis Park, and Uptown Minneapolis.

INTRODUCTION

The event host says, "You have two to five minutes to introduce yourself."

You immediately think:

1. *Oh, that's way too long; what will I say for two to five minutes?*
2. *Perfect amount of time. I'll even try to cut it short.*
3. *That's not enough time. I wish I had more.*

No matter which one of the three groups you fall into, my guess is it is highly unlikely you will limit your speaking to five minutes or less. In fact, there is a good chance you may even become unfocused. You'll find your brain not quite able to organize your thoughts on the spot, not quite able to magically formulate what will eventually come out of your mouth. So what does come out lacks a clear goal. How do I know? Partly because I've spent my entire career as a professional communicator, and I've seen the exact scenario play out—sometimes in my own performance and lots of times with people around me. I started doing commercial talent work when I was in my late teens and early twenties. These were scripted ads or videos, which I had to deliver with authority and authenticity. Plus, I couldn't take my own sweet time. I was on the clock.

Eventually, I launched my professional career in television news. Live and taped reports multiple times a day for nearly a decade make one learn how to convey a message with crisp and interesting language. TV news, more than most media outlets, doesn't give a person much time to deliver the story. I had to learn how to condense an eight- to twelve-hour day's worth of work into a report of about one to three minutes on air. No time for rambling. And when I was doing a live report (versus a pre-recorded one), I also had to be ready to ad lib about whatever my anchor threw at me, not to mention whatever a random passerby might throw on me. During one taping, a baby camel I was feeding even decided to spit up on me—its spit not necessarily landing on the ground, if you know what I mean.

Now as a communication consultant, I train and coach people how to get to their WOW! by presenting their best. How to take themselves from their current state of comfort and ability as a presenter, what I call their now, and get moving toward their most powerful communicator self, their WOW! As vocal talent, I use my own voice and experience as a speaker to connect with listeners. The audience can't see me, so my ability to deliver through vocal behavior alone is key. I not only feel comfortable in front of a microphone or a crowd, I welcome challenges to my presentation comfort zones. But I didn't get this way overnight. In every performance setting I encountered, my comfort level increased only through repetition. Believe me when I say, unless you have gotten used to what speaking for a minute feels like, you inevitably will speak for longer than a minute or two or five. But don't worry; your preparation doesn't require a media career.

The communication process of any kind involves self-awareness and self-knowledge. That goes for a two- to five-minute introduction as well as for a State of the Union Address. In the real world, unless your audience is your mom or someone else who loves you a lot, most people do not want to hear you talk for hours or even minutes on end. If you are giving an introduction or even a keynote, do you really think you should be speaking stream-of-consciousness, starting with where you were born and ending with what you had for lunch today?

So how do you self-edit? It's not rocket science but does require some forethought. Ask yourself whether you have a plan. If you don't, you need one. If you know you need one but don't know how to create the plan, try to think of it as a fun game. I will help you make the entire experience an easy process with a communication formula I created.

THE I-A-P™ FORMULA GOES PUBLIC

I have a name for this process—the **I-A-P™** Formula. I lay it all out in detail throughout this book. For now, let me introduce you to this friendly little formula—built to help you get over any presentation or communication challenges:

I = Intent

A = Audience Analysis

P = Powerful Performance

If you can put aside your angst and hesitation and just focus on this process for becoming a better communicator, the **I-A-P™** Formula will help you get to your WOW!

First, I will show you how to put a label on the impact you want to leave. And that label will enable you to be more productive in your preparation and effective with your final result. I ask you as I ask my clients, "What's your **Intent** (I) with this presentation?"

Second, you will determine whether you are in a professional setting, a social setting, or a mixed setting. I'll teach you how to figure out what kind of people you are presenting to in that setting. In other words, you'll do a little **Audience Analysis** (A).

Third, and this is key, aim to leave your audience wanting more. The most successful communicators have a way of making ten minutes seem like two, and they give you the notion you could listen to them for hours. Much of this comes from how they present. **Powerful Performance** (P) will help you deliver the content of your presentation moment well and help you leave an impression on your audience. Why would you go through all the work of planning a presentation just to lose it in your delivery? I often say it doesn't really matter what you know, if you don't know how to present it.

The **I-A-P™** Formula is a noun. It is a thing—a process. However, you may occasionally see me using it as a verb—suggesting you **I-A-P™** it. I'm not trying to be grammatically incorrect. To help you view the formula as a process, I will easily use it as an action verb. I want to draw you into doing something proactive to improve on your ability to communicate well.

I-A-P™ DEFINITIONS

Some terms to help you get the most out of this book:

Presentation Moment	any communication setting—whether with one person or a group of any size; live or recorded
Self-Perception	how you view yourself
Toolbox	your new set of presentation skills
Toolbox Talk	a recap of key points at the end of each chapter
Less is More	my favorite saying—helpful with self-editing
Authentic	your identified or real personality, traits, comfort zone
Image	your overall appearance, including face, hair, wardrobe
Vocal Behavior	the tone, sound, and subtext of your voice and how your delivery is received/perceived by others
Audience	the people to whom you present—one or many; will hear you, see you, or both
WOW!	the end result of applying your toolbox of skills to a communication goal and achieving it; keep in mind, your WOW! is a moving target

WHY I-A-P™?

Remember, the **I-A-P™** Formula is your friend. It is meant to make presentation moments more fun and manageable. My goal with **I-A-P™** is to give you a road map so you can focus on the communication process instead of on any fears about presenting or apprehension about accomplishing your objectives.

I-A-P™ ANYTIME, ANYWHERE

You will eventually get to a place as a communicator where you don't need to be so focused on every detail of the **I-A-P™** process. But even when you get to that place, and I'll cheer that day, you will want to use the formula. I tell my clients to run any presentation moment through an **I-A-P™** check at an early stage in their preparation. If you don't have answers, you'll get them. If you do have answers, you'll fine-tune what you already know and come off looking and sounding even better.

Let's get started on the road to your WOW!

SECTION I

INTENT

Why Am I Here Anyway?

CHAPTER 1

TOTALLY COMMIT OR DON'T EVEN BOTHER

Some people are commitment phobic. We joke about this when it comes to romantic relationships. But commitment is no laughing matter when it comes to your presentation moments. If you aren't committed to what you hope to accomplish and what you're going to say, things will go haywire fast. So how do you get over the commitment jitters and get started? Think of this commitment as the beginning of a beautiful relationship. That relationship is the launching of your Intent process. And just as in any dating game, you'll face expectations along the way. Knowing *who's* expecting *what* will help you formulate what you, the presenter, want and need to do.

PRESENTER EXPECTATIONS

You might say, "My expectations? That's easy. I just want to do a good job." Great, but try to be more specific. Really ask yourself why you chose this presentation moment. Why you let yourself be in this specific place at this specific time. Is there something about the audience that jazzes you? Is this a non-profit you wish to shower with your expertise? Do you hope to make an impression on this type of professional group because you want future clients as a direct result? If you don't know why you're there, how do you expect your audience to know? Or really gain anything from what you present?

You'll find I treat each part of the I-A-P™ Formula as co-equal. But the Intent stage is the driver that helps make the other parts more successful. I devote section II to Audience Analysis, but starting to think about your audience's expectations here at the Intent stage will help you formulate a more focused intent for any presentation moment.

AUDIENCE EXPECTATIONS

And speaking of your audience, each and every member in it will come with his or her own expectations. Accept the fact that audience members bring a diversity of preferences to your presentation. But at the end, you want most people to land at the same place, or at least within the firing zone. You are the guide to get them there.

Who Brought You?

One way to figure out audience expectations is to remember who invited you to present. If it's a corporation that's putting on a big conference, and your presentation is one workshop in the entire day, then let that fact guide you and ask some questions before you prepare. If you're the keynote speaker, then you have an inspirational expectation attached to whatever content you deliver. Did you just win the Nobel Prize for physics, and your audience is a bunch of non-science people? Just as there are all kinds of intent, there are various expectations you must consider.

For example, when Big Brothers-Big Sisters asked me to emcee its first annual awards luncheon in Minneapolis, I thought about why the organization asked me. I figured: They knew about my background in TV news. They knew I currently do radio. They knew I handle ad-lib scenarios well. They needed someone who could handle quieting the audience when necessary, deliver their pre-written awards luncheon script, ad-lib in order to make the words my own, and introduce a dynamic keynote speaker they'd flown in from New York City. My expectations for myself were so intertwined with the planners' expectations; I had no problem committing to what was needed. I knew I had to deliver a smooth performance. That analysis helped me go about preparing for the big day with a clear focus in mind. And if you're ever at a loss for what's expected of you, ask your event planner or host.

Why Are You Special?

Another area for audience expectation analysis is to think about who you are. Do you sit on several corporate boards, and your impressive resume makes you an interesting or sought-after presenter to this particular group? If so, they likely want you to share some stories and help those in the audience who aspire to attain achievements like yours get some solid information. Are you a professional or college athlete-turned financial consultant? You may be the main speaker at an event because of how you transitioned. Your big-name past likely got you on their radar, so this audience may want you to share some stories from your athletic career.

Identifying why you, and you in particular, are here helps you commit to the content, your audience, and to a specific intent. You really must totally commit to carrying out a specific intent. You and your audience will thank you.

TOOLBOX TALK*

1. **Know who expects what**
2. **Define your own reasons for wanting/needing to be here**
3. **Understand your audience's expectations**

**Toolbox Talk will greet you at the end of each chapter to summarize some key points.*

CHAPTER 2

SIZE DOES MATTER

You might think I'm just trying to get a giggle by referencing a common size joke most of us have heard. But really, I'm actually mentioning something we've all heard, laughed about, or pondered in order to get across an important point. Size does matter. But big, small, or medium isn't the point. In order to be a powerful communicator in every presentation moment, you must deal with the size of your audience when you're figuring out your intent for being in front of them. In other words, *before* you get in front of them.

Part two of the I-A-P™ Formula deals with Audience Analysis. I will get into more detailed speaking tips and devices for any size audience in the next section. For now, here at the Intent stage, you need to identify the size of your group before you actually present in front of your audience. That will help you put yourself in position to come up with the best intent for your presentation moment to come. Identifying the size of the audience will help you streamline and cater your content to their needs. You deliver differently based on the audience size—intimate versus general. So help yourself by realizing that your intent may change as the size of your crowd does. Size does matter. And it matters very much that you know what you're dealing with before you delve too deeply into structuring your presentation moment.

ONE-ON-ONE

Many people are most comfortable when the only audience they have is one person. If you know you're comfortable with the singular setting, then figuring out your intent for this oh-so-intimate of audiences should be a snap. But in business settings, it's important you don't allow yourself to get a false comfort or complacency just because your group is not a group but rather a solo spectator.

Planning your intent for the one-on-one situation should be celebrated as an opportunity to really showcase yourself. Showcase your ability to truly tune in to your audience and shape an intent that makes the person feel like you only care about his or her needs. It's important to narrow down your intent for this size audience and keep your examples and anecdotes zeroed in on your solo spectator's needs and wishes.

Fine-tune your intent and really make it work for you. Is your person a runner or golfer? Fashion an intent that makes your presentation examples relate to his or her passions. Relax but don't take the pressure off yourself just because you're speaking to one and not dozens or hundreds.

An example of a one-on-one audience in my world as a consultant is the individual executive, business owner, or author. My audience is one in these cases, but I must spend time with the I-A-P™ Formula to ensure I give my client a thorough training. In determining the intent for any solo client session, I'm thinking about particular styles and presentation goals. Not all executives have the same presentation goals. And not all authors face the same challenges when they get interviewed by the media. So I keep each individual client in mind—the person's strengths and needs—as I figure out a particular intent for a particular session. If I get too wrapped up with thinking about all salespeople as a group or all business owners as a bunch, I can't truly formulate an intent that will help this one particular client in the one particular day with this one particular presentation issue. It's actually a comfort *not* to have to worry about all authors when I'm preparing to train one particular author who just wrote a book about walnuts and now wants help sounding interesting in a TV interview. If I thought about a different author client who writes about skydiving, that won't help this particular person with the walnut interview. When I can focus on the one author's needs, I'm able to pull from my content and deliver instruction that will end in a positive result for this author.

SMALL GROUP

Once you start counting above one, you start bumping into the small groups. A small group may number three for some and thirty for others. No matter what size you label your small group, go ahead and label it. Definitely decide what a small group means to you. This will help you prepare your mind for how to start preparing your intent. For me, a small group is five to fifty. Locking that in helps me focus and come up with the right intent for this particular presentation moment in front of this particular audience.

Zoning in on this small group and its actual number of people helps define reality and helps you subcategorize within your small group. When you have five people, you might do something differently than you would with a small group of twenty-five. Figuring out at the Intent stage what you could do with small groups and their subcategories puts you in a position to prepare better. Whether it's the use of interactive components in your talk or the number of handouts you'll need, defining and labeling the audience as a small group can also be a sense of comfort. After all, you're not going to be in front of a group of five hundred; you're speaking in front of fifty people. That should sound less intimidating.

You also can identify what is logistically possible within your venue space and that, in turn, helps you figure out how to deliver what you intend to deliver content-wise. Will you do Q&A with the audience? With five people, you don't have to worry about microphones and being heard compared to a small group of thirty. Based on the numbers, you can figure out ahead of time what kind of personalization you can do with your small group. I give keynotes as part of my business offerings. Most I do for a fee. Every once in awhile I will do a keynote for a reduced fee or trade if the organization is one I believe in, has no speaker budget, *and* presents a great marketing opportunity. I find these marketing opportunity settings great occasions to put some twists on some of my material, especially when the talk is in front of a small group. In every instance, I ask my host to identify people in the small group, either by name or profession, so I can use the information to formulate my intent for the particular presentation moment.

If I know I'm speaking to a mixed industry group of business people about media skills, I want to have a sense of who the audience is made up of in order to prepare content those diverse industries can understand.

LARGE GROUP

Large group audiences seem to scare many people. I say congratulate yourself if you are preparing to present to a large group. Someone believes you're up to the task, and everyone in the audience expects you to be. Use this as a time to shine and highlight yourself and your professionalism. There's no better feeling than to come out of a presentation of any kind feeling like you connected with your audience. You feel like your audience really heard you, like you really taught them something. What a natural high! I will always wish this for you.

Just as with the small group, identify and then label what a large group means to you. To my client, the owner of a national gourmet food company, speaking in front of thousands of sales consultants is a regular part of her work life. To the latest Superbowl winners, a stadium full of tens of thousands of fans is a large group versus signing autographs in the children's ward at a hospital. Whatever the number, identify it for yourself. Then realize you can take the best from your one-on-one and small group intent preparation and formulate it for a large group. You do want to make people within the large group feel like you are talking with them individually. There lies the similarity with the one-on-one performance. Use this factor as your security blanket. This is a skill you can learn. I'll get into more details in the next section on Audience Analysis but for now, don't jump over defining your intent with this large group.

You figure for a rock star who sings in front of fifty thousand fans, the intent is to use the adrenaline of a large crowd to make the crowd feel they're part of something special. The intent is to entertain and touch people. The rock star uses group momentum to even more powerfully connect with audience members on an individual level. But success won't come unless the rock star goes onstage with some idea of the mission with this particular large group. And he or she can't treat this one large group in Dallas the same way a large group in Minneapolis is treated. Do you ever notice how a lot of singers will say, "Hello, Houston!"? They certainly wouldn't greet a large group in San Antonio with that line, even though the cities are in the same state. The smart rock star realizes that city to city, region to region, even audience to audience, it's critical to create a singular intent for *this* performance.

And that is the point. *This* audience, no matter how large, is made up of individuals. Don't forget that, and your Intent plan for large group audiences becomes more manageable and easier to visualize. Too often when faced with a large group, the presenter suddenly feels he or she is in front of a big organism and doesn't really connect with anyone. Instead, remember you are in front of a group that's made up of multiple individuals. They will each receive you independently even though you present to them all at once.

Now that you're empowered with focused information about why you're here and who your audience is, you're in a good place to get inspired by your content and inspire others with your intent.

TOOLBOX TALK

1. **Label your group size**
2. **Decide what this client/group needs**
3. **No matter the size, remember the group is made up of individuals**

CHAPTER 3

YOUR INTENT AS A ROAD MAP

You may wonder why I'm so adamant about intent. Once you have your intent defined, the rest becomes more guided and controllable. Think of intent as a road map—a road map to your presentation moment. Unlike maps you buy at the store, this one you create. You set it in motion by defining your intent at the beginning of your preparation stage. Your intent can be specific, or it might be general. The sky is literally the limit when it comes to intent. But the important part is that you identify *what* your intent actually is. The more identifiable your intent is to you, the more likely your chance for overall success. You'll have more focus and be better equipped to prepare content that can accomplish your goals for this presentation moment. Let's explore some likely areas of intent.

INSPIRE—LET'S GO SKYDIVING

Sometimes the goal in front of you is not specific. Your goal or the goal of the person who asked you to present is this: inspire the crowd. That instruction is a wide open canvas. A more generic intent may also be scary to some presenters. But let's break it up.

What makes for the most powerful performances? A simple concept—authenticity. The most comfortable and successful speakers are those who *know who they are*, and they *know what they know*. The moment you forget these two integral concepts is when the road map heads into undesirable territory. You're probably thinking who forgets who they are? I'll tell you—anyone and everyone. Big-title people as well as regular business people working their way up the career ladder often lose basic self-knowledge when in front of an audience. Many business people get tied up in knots when they are on the spot in a presentation moment. They may even turn into some formal version of themselves that's not at all relatable to the audience. So if you need to inspire your audience, the chances of success slip away quickly because you don't have an authentic place from which to inspire.

If your intent for this presentation moment is to inspire, you must start with your authentic self. From there, ask yourself what's interesting to you. Ask yourself what you get passionate about. Are you an avid skydiver? Do you have a talent for getting people to give up their fears and take a leap? Then skydiving's a topic about which you're well-suited to inspire. You may have a less fun topic than skydiving ahead of you. You can still use your high-flying hobby as your inspiration. Draw on the skydiving passion to formulate your intent to inspire. Are there analogies you can make between the topic at hand and your thorough knowledge of skydiving? Use that data. A mistake many people make when they're faced with a presentation moment is they forget about their own lives—both in and out of work. Your life is a great place from which to draw stories and quotes that you can weave into your presentation topic. And when you are able to connect tangible aspects of your life into your presentation moments, you can't help but inspire others.

EDUCATE—WELCOME TO SCHOOL

Perhaps the goal in front of you is to educate. Again, don't forget *who you are* or *what you know*. Even with this more informative intent, your life gives you a breeding ground for good ideas, relatable stories, and identifiable examples of how what you are going to talk about can help educate your audience. The important focus here is that you define and embrace your intent. You are trying to educate. That doesn't mean you need to get robotic. I often see business people turn into rigid versions of themselves when they're out to educate. Think back. You've seen it. And you likely were bored or not persuaded by their content. Perhaps you were even distracted by their lack of personality. You do need to understand that the goal of educating your audience requires you to break things down in more detail than you might with most other intents while at the same time keeping your natural humanity. If you're supposed to teach a group of eighteen-year-olds about first aid and CPR, you must use words and activities that show them how to do new activities. You are not *inspiring* them to save a life. You are *educating* them about real medical practices.

One of my clients is an excellent example. He's general manager at a country club. He heard me give a keynote titled "Who Are You?" This keynote is one of the talks I give under my *From Now to WOW!*™ presentation training programs. The keynote was about thirty minutes in front of a group of eighty business people. My presentation apparently inspired this general manager to walk up to me post-talk and ask me about coming in to train his management team and other select employees—a wonderful result for most speakers. My goal to inspire the crowd to think about the importance of making a good impression seemed to work with this particular gentleman. He was inspired by my call to action about making sure you strive to make good impressions and decided his team could use some additional skills to market themselves and the country club better.

But as I planned the customized training for the country club team a few months later, my intent changed from what it had been for the keynote. The intent went from inspire to educate with this group. Their GM wanted his team to learn specific skills to help them do their jobs more powerfully. Even though the training covered more topical ground than the keynote, it also required a different intent on my part to fulfill the need of this different audience.

Had I stayed wrapped up in the same mindset as I had with the "Who Are You?" keynote, I would not have given myself a proper road map for meeting this general manager's expectations. Before I could do anything else, I had to identify my intent for this group of people. That gave me the right mindset to create a road map and then navigate it.

ENTERTAIN—YOU MAKE ME WANT TO DANCE

Another kind of intent is one that gives you a lot of room for creativity. To entertain is divine. For those of us with an inner comedian, the entertain intent allows for a great deal of freedom. If your plan, your boss's directive, or your client's objective is for you to get up there and entertain, I suggest you embrace the fact that you have so much room to be authentic. You have so much space to have fun with yourself and with your audience. You are the only obstacle to a WOW! moment.

When you're asked to entertain, you can use a lot of things you wouldn't, or perhaps couldn't, use with other intents. You could juggle at the opening of your presentation moment. You could start your presentation moment with a crazy movie clip or video montage set to music. These techniques may be appropriate for other intents to be sure, but you probably wouldn't let yourself have as much fun with these launching pads unless your intent is to entertain. Whatever ultimately gets you through the content and is cohesive can work. I urge you to let yourself go when your intent is to entertain. In fact, people retain more information when they are entertained. Have fun with this intent.

COMBINE INTENTS—THE BALANCING ACT

You may one day find yourself with a multi-dimensional or dual-purpose intent. Do not lose control. Do not freak out. You can handle this. You're just facing a road map with a few more twists and turns. I suggest you first decide if there's an overarching *main* intent and one or more additional goals. Or, do you have a combination of intents that is of equal importance?

The best situation is when you have one intent you can focus all your efforts. But life doesn't always follow the map. When that happens, apply some of the rules in this chapter and think of balance. Remain calm and give yourself a focus with each intent. Maybe one part of your presentation calls for you to educate and another points to the goal of inspiring. Balance will be the key to creating a road map when faced with more than a singular intent.

Much like excellent, strong presentation moments, intents that build road maps get better with practice. I focus the next chapter on helping you get some inspiration in finding the right intent. Travel forward.

TOOLBOX TALK

1. Intent drives the road map for your presentation moment
2. Be authentic
3. Ask yourself, "Do I know who I am?"
4. Ask yourself, "Do I know what I know?"
5. Intent can be general or specific

CHAPTER 4

SOURCE OF INSPIRATION

By now, you should have your road map in place. Your road map is important because it guides your entire presentation moment. But how do you ignite the right energy to get you moving through your road map to make sure every word that comes out of your mouth actually says something? How do you make sure your examples are relevant and enlightening? How do you accomplish your intent?

You look for a source of inspiration on your road to creating a truly winning presentation. There are several techniques I share with my clients and use in my own presentation moments to get in the right frame of mind to accomplish my intent goals. These techniques can be your inspiration to action.

INTERACTION

You've seen 'em. They're presenters who are glued to their podium and never appear comfortable unless they are two hundred feet away from their audience. Or they speak at you but don't make the content relevant to you. Yes, they're even robotic.

You've probably also seen presenters who inspire you, who involve their audience in the material, and make the time fly. This is the kind of communicator I want you to become. Interaction with your audience is a proactive way to grow into that kind of presenter.

Simple Steps for Interaction

There are some simple methods for interaction. For instance, you can call someone by name and ask a direct question. How about sharing an anecdote that involves someone in the audience? Of course, make sure it's not something confidential or embarrassing. For instance, I would never ask someone about their weight, whether they use a hairpiece, or if they're pregnant. People love to hear the sound of their own name, though. Use this to your advantage. You are interacting with your audience and specifically speaking to whomever you include in the story whenever you include names of audience members. By interacting in this way, you are actually addressing *one* person while you speak to the entire group. You are connecting on multiple levels with your audience. I rarely see an audience member who doesn't like this kind of individual attention during the course of a presentation. And when that person is the subject of your story or anecdote, he or she walks away from your presentation moment feeling even more involved. He or she will remember you better.

Those you did *not* call on will remember you in a more productive and complete way too. They witnessed you as the type of presenter who's comfortable enough to interact with the audience. It always amazes me how impressed people are with interaction. I often get comments from people along these lines: "I can't believe you remembered so many people's names." Or, "I really like how you related a story to my company and singled me out with questions and comments." Simple techniques can go a long way.

Less Simple but Effective Interaction Techniques

There are certainly more elaborate methods for interaction at your disposal. They are as complex as you can dream up. You can interact with a table of people. You can get the entire room to stand up. One example of that for me is when I invite everyone to stand up and do some vocal exercises. I'll go over those exercises with you in coming chapters.

You can choreograph how any interactive moments will look ahead of time. You could practice with your colleagues. All of these interactive steps can help you carry out your intent more thoroughly and successfully. They can also mean the difference between a passive audience member and someone who visits with you post-performance wanting to hire you or your company.

My intent is to make things easier and less overwhelming for you as a presenter. Let me share some types of interaction with an intermediate level of difficulty. I label them intermediate because they require some focus. You must keep control of your presentation flow while at the same time incorporate another or others into that presentation. For example, *script* in some interaction moments for any presentation you give. Actually plan them into your agenda, then call up someone or people from the audience to help you with one or more parts of your content. I like to think of these audience members as human models that help demonstrate the material. In some cases, you may tell them ahead of time you will do this. Other times, you're going for spontaneity because you don't want the human models to over-think what's ahead and perhaps mess up your opportunity to make a certain point.

I'll share an example from one of my presentation moments. When I give a *From Now to WOW!*™ keynote or training, we get into image work. Image, as I teach it, involves face, hair, and wardrobe. There are exercises in all of those areas I do with individual consulting clients during any one-on-one setting with them. But when I have a small or large group in front of me, I use the same ideas and concepts and essentially try to make it feel like an individual consult. By having an interactive moment with one audience member as a human model, I bring my material to life. People remember what they see a lot better than what they hear. And showing is more effective than just telling them my teachings about face, hair, and wardrobe.

Here's an interaction moment I like to use. One aspect of using the face in communication is understanding presentation assets you possess right on your face. Some people don't know they have them. Others recognize these assets but don't use them. Bring in the human model. When I invite a volunteer (i.e., someone I just call on randomly) to the front of the room, I ask, "What's your best facial feature?" You see how I am interacting with the human model individually. But I also ask the audience to answer the same question about my human model and write the answer down in their notes. In a larger sense, I'm interacting with the group in that way too. We have lots of fun reviewing the human volunteer's answers as well as the audience response.

This human model method of interaction can be as simple or as intricate as you'd like. The goal is to know you will use an interaction moment or moments as you shape your intent for this presentation moment. Let the fact that you're going to interact with your audience be your inspiration to more clearly define your intent.

LESS IS MORE

A phrase my clients and students often hear from me is *less is more.* It really sums up things. Sometimes too much of a good thing can make things bad. Too much ice cream makes you sick. Too much of one color in a rainbow ruins the entire image. And too many words or ideas in a presentation moment jeopardizes your ability to make your point effectively.

But how do you get to less without removing too much? How do you present more in a streamlined succinct manner? First, be sure to keep your time constraints in mind. When you are setting your intent and using *less is more* as your source of inspiration, be sure you're figuring out what you want to accomplish with a keen sense of the clock. Topics usually always take more time to present than we think. When you're in the actual presentation moment with an audience in front of you, you probably take more time to get the words out than when you practiced in front of a mirror.

When I give my "Who Are You?" talk to a group of business people, I try to show each participant how to reach a WOW! in his or her personal introduction. The final thing each person in the group has to do during this training is prepare an introduction using the I-A-P™ Formula. Then I select several people to perform their introductions for the group. They each are asked to showcase use of the formula and ultimately perform with flair. During one particularly memorable group talk, a gentleman got to redo his introduction and presented much better after a little feedback. But, ultimately, he was able to clarify his intent for himself before he re-did his introduction for the group.

Another time, one woman had a fairly decent introduction, but near what should have been the end of it, she paused and seemed flustered as she started to continue. She looked at me for help. I said, "Why don't you just stop there?" She did, and with the group I covered how *less is more* inspiration could have helped her plan her introduction better. She had a loose intent and a stream-of-consciousness method to her performance. Had she let *less is more* inspire her, she may have planned out what she was going to say more effectively.

Many times people think they need to pack everything into whatever presentation assignment is in front of them. They think they won't convince anyone of anything if they leave out even one detail. The problem with that? Usually too much content is a killer for coherence and clarity. Visualize using language for your presentation moment that consists of declarative sentences with periods. Do not use rambling thoughts that would contain lots of commas, if you were to write out your sentence. Can you see the difference in your mind before you open your mouth?

One favorite example of *less is more* inspiration actually comes from a story about a written document. One of my attorney clients was to argue in front of her state supreme court. She had to write a brief for the court prior to the argument stage. The weekend before the brief was due, she found out the brief was limited to twenty pages. This was an issue because she was approaching one hundred pages with her legal brief. Somewhere along the line, she hadn't fully realized the rules of that court for that particular brief. But she didn't fall apart. She let herself be inspired.

She left me a message, "Roshini, you're going to appreciate this *less is more* story." Ultimately, she had to cut seventy pages from her brief to fulfill the court's rules. She shared more details about what a good exercise in *less is more* that was for her. She really had to pin down the intent of her legal brief. Clarity with her intent helped her focus the road map, which ultimately helped her write the condensed version.

THE AUDIENCE

Believe it or not, your audience can be a source of inspiration to help you formulate the best intent for your presentation moment. Your knowledge of them is relevant for your intent. Audience analysis is one segment of the I-A-P™ Formula. But here at the intent stage, you should use your knowledge of your audience to get a sense of what they can handle or what they can't. For example, if you have a room full of bankers, your intent is unlikely to include a review of common math. However, if a group of first graders is your audience, lessons about addition or subtraction may be appropriate.

Take that group of bankers and put them at their summer golf outing. Your intent on that day is likely to be a little softer—less hard-hitting on content. In the next section, I'll give you a more detailed way to analyze your audience as you continue to build your road map.

TOOLBOX TALK

1. **Interaction makes you more real and can inspire you to create the intent for any particular audience**
2. **Human models help you solidify and clarify**
3. **The *less is more* concept can help you edit and focus your intent/content**
4. **Remembering who your audience is helps you focus your intent**

SECTION II

AUDIENCE ANALYSIS

Who Are These People?

CHAPTER 5

SET THE SCENE

I like to say I'm Roshini every day. I'm Roshini for my mother. I'm Roshini for my clients. I'm Roshini for my friends. I stay the same, but my audience changes. I don't want to, or need to, change who I am just because my audience changes. But I do want to be effective no matter who's in front of me—whether that be live or in front of a screen. A crucial part of being successful as a communicator is to understand that each audience has needs. Along with that, each member of that audience has needs and reasons for taking in your content. Sometimes you may get a similar audience possessing varying needs. Let's take bankers for instance. You may think what you did with those bankers yesterday you can do again for this group of bankers today. Think again, my friend.

Audience Analysis is the second part of the I-A-P™ Formula but just as important as the first. Do you want to figure out how to do what you need to do in order to make each presentation moment a WOW! for any audience while at the same time *not* changing who you are to get there? If you don't, you should. If you do, great. I can help you no matter which way you answer now.

There are three different arenas from which you may draw your audience. To help you be a more comfortable presenter in any situation, try to figure out ahead of time in which group your particular audience fits. That identification will then help as you perform your content with help from the final part of the I-A-P™ Formula.

THE PROFESSIONAL AUDIENCE

Are you talking to people who are in, and expect to be in, a business setting and know each other *only* in a business context? Will risky jokes be treated with frowns and dropped jaws? Do you need to make a great impression for future business dealings? If you answered yes to any of these questions, you are dealing with an audience that's solely professional. You may have some friends in the group, but you must treat the professional audience as just that—professional. This doesn't mean you turn into a formal version of yourself. But you realize this group doesn't necessarily know you're a mother with three kids. Or they don't realize you're a father who coaches hockey for the local high school.

When you're able to identify your audience as purely professional, you can draw from certain areas of your content and not others. For example, you can comfortably quote *Fortune* magazine but perhaps not the Bible. I liken the professional audience to my viewers when I was in television news. As a news reporter, I was the neutral. I had to make sure all sides in a story got representation without seeming biased toward any one of them. I also was careful on days that I knew I'd be at work, and therefore on TV, to *not* wear jewelry that might seem to favor one political party or another or anything that might broadcast any idea about my own religious beliefs.

The professional audience is usually an easy one to spot. But it helps to identify it as you go through the I-A-P™ Formula in order to make your presentation planning easier and more focused.

THE SOCIAL AUDIENCE

Most of us are lucky enough to get away from our work and hang out with people or groups that are focused on something social: a book club, a basketball league, a close-knit yoga class. This audience is one in front of which you can be more relaxed because you're not necessarily thinking about business while you're with them. I won't spend a lot of time on this kind of audience because it's the least related to business settings and my focus in this book. But it's important to identify the *social* audience as you go through your I-A-P™ analysis. There will be times when you have business dealings in front of a purely social audience. I expect you are now in a better position to understand how you can still accomplish your business goals if that social encounter requires a business function from you.

For example, I bought Girl Scout cookies from one of my neighbor's children. When I went to deliver my check, the mom asked me about my business. She ended up wanting more information because she believed her company could use my consulting services. During football season, I was with the Boston College Club of Minnesota watching our beloved Eagles play our big rival Notre Dame. I expected it would be an afternoon of football and food. In addition, some business talk ensued when a fellow alum asked me about media training for the charitable organization she oversees. I've even had business prospects approach me at the gym. You never know when these presentation possibilities might happen, but you will always feel empowered if you know they could. And further, it behooves you to be ready for presentation moments in social settings.

THE MIXED AUDIENCE *(Professional + Social)*

Sometimes you are in a business setting, but you have many friends or acquaintances in that setting. You have several people about whom you know many personal details. Or it's an organization you've belonged to for many years, and you've formed friendships with several other members. You look forward to seeing them, and both sides have an interest in one another beyond work in general and that organization in particular.

The *mixed* audience can be the most rewarding of the audiences you face during your presentation moments, but it might also prove the most challenging for you to prepare. In any mixed audience, you are on varying levels of familiarity with separate members of the audience. You have to treat the audience as one group, but you know there are people in the audience who know you fairly well. There are also audience members who are strangers. So you must find the balance in how you present to the group. You do not want to insult anyone or make anyone feel left out, while at the same time get your message across to everyone with clarity and authority.

Once you identify that you will be in front of a mixed audience, look at other factors to help you further refine your analysis. Is this a Chamber of Commerce? Is it an industry association, like the National Realtors of America? Is it a small group of sales people from various industries to whom you are pitching your services? Get a sense of the different layers of mixed that are going on with this mixed audience. Awareness of every level of differentiation can help you formulate your content to appeal to a broader range that encompasses those who know you and those who don't. Consider the ones you are more familiar with as a security blanket. Think of them as easy people to interact with during your presentation. They are people you can call on if you decide to use questions within your talk. The less familiar people in the audience shouldn't feel neglected because some or much of your content remains valuable and interesting to them too.

Now that you have some tools to help you identify your audience and set the scene for their needs, you should go further and deeper in your audience analysis to really shine. Organize your audience research into three parts. Just as a presentation moment or a movie has a beginning, middle, and end, your background reconnaissance on this audience starts *before* you present to them, continues *during* your presentation moment, and winds down *after* you leave them.

We will start with the *before* stage in the next chapter.

TOOLBOX TALK

1. **Identify the type of audience**
2. **There are three major audience types:**

   -Professional = know only in business context

   -Social = invites more of a relaxed atmosphere, e.g., bowling leagues, book clubs

   -Mixed = Professional + Social

CHAPTER 6

BEFORE THE SHOW

Now that you've identified the nature of your audience, it's time to go into more detail with your Audience Analysis. Remembering the I-A-P™ Formula, you'll recall we are in the middle part or the "A" section of our planning. Within this section, there are three parts to Audience Analysis—before, during, and after. First, you must start with what happens *before* your presentation moment. Or as I like to call it, *before the show.*

At this stage, you can do all the homework you want on your audience. They are not in front of you. There are no time crunches unless you create them. So ask yourself a few questions and get the answers through research. Research may involve looking things up online, talking with your sponsor or client, actually chatting with members you are familiar with from the group before show time. You can ask questions of others and yourself as you seek out background information. Some questions include:

- *What are some of the organizations represented in this audience?*
- *What kinds of work do they do and oversee?*
- *What are the names of people who would be comfortable to get called on directly by me during any interactive moment?*
- *What are the pressing issues in the industry or industries these people belong?*

Let me share some specific areas to research and preview that will help you really understand the audience that will be in front of you.

WHO

No matter what, ask yourself: *Who* are these people? Who can be a general question, or it can be specific. At this point, you want to focus and be specific. You know the presentation setting ahead; you've started figuring out your intent for the upcoming presentation moment. Now, you really figure out who will be your audience. Are they doctors, shareholders, bartenders, flight attendants? Do they work in the education arena? Will athletes be mixed in if it's a group of coaches?

You can also use some of the information you gathered from the specific questions listed in the opening to this chapter to get at the heart of *this* audience.

IDENTIFY PROFESSION—MIXED OR SAME?

Taking the *who* question one step further, you will want to know if you're going to be in front of a group that's homogenous or mixed. Do you have all bankers? Or do you have some bankers, some accountants, and some underwriters? The answer to this question will help you focus your material and make any interactive elements you use more relatable.

AGE/GENDER MIX

Going deeper, how old, or roughly how old, are the members of your audience? Are they all women? Are they all men or does the audience contain both men and women? Figuring out the age and gender mix will help you decide which examples to use and which levels of humor are appropriate. Some jokes or examples may alienate an age group or even an entire gender. I'll let you imagine those examples. But it's always a good idea to figure this out ahead of time and up to you to respect and know your audience to your best ability as you prepare.

THEIR NEEDS, NOT YOURS

A needs assessment requires some pointed reflection from you before you're in front of your audience. You have your intent locked down by now. But ask yourself what your audience really wants to get out of your content. If you need a little assistance figuring this out, do some research. Communicate with the person bringing you in and ask questions to help you get answers. Perhaps that conversation happens with more than one person. Find out why you got selected over other options. You may find your intended audience is impressed with a book you recently wrote and wants to hear about the experiences you lived. You never know unless you ask. And asking will bring you information that will help make you infinitely more successful in front of your audience, partly because you carried out the mission given to you, but also because you help make the person who brought you in look good.

FIGURE OUT COMMONALITIES AMONG AUDIENCE MEMBERS

You may have a group of one hundred people made up of three related industries. Now, go deeper and figure out if there are some things that tie them together that aren't necessarily job-specific. Perhaps they're all or mostly all parents. Maybe Bank #1 just closed a huge deal with Underwriter Company #3, and they're both in your audience. If this is public information and positive news, intertwine an anecdote about this into your talk.

Commonalities between and among specific segments of your audience can help you. This is one area you can mine to personalize your content. The more direct and connected to any audience you can structure your material, the better your chances of success fulfilling objectives and getting repeat appearances.

FIND ANY CONNECTIONS TO YOU

This might prove to be an interesting and rewarding detail for you. It may also help you get over jitters and be highly effective. Find out if you personally know anyone who's going to be in your audience. A related question is to find out if there are any people in the audience who have connections to groups you are a part of or associations to which you belong. If audience members do have connections to you, you can identify these connections naturally throughout your talk. You can call on individual people randomly and expect them to willingly respond and make you seem even more like a rock star. Audience members, even the shier ones, like to hear their own names. And if you showcase your connection to specific people in this audience, you make them seem and feel like rock stars.

Several times I've given keynotes at The Woman's Club of Minneapolis. I enjoy business events at the club and have made many friends there. That's part of the reason I enjoy speaking in front of club audiences. I also have several friends and clients who are members of the club. This helps me personalize stories during keynotes I deliver at club events. I can be more effective as a speaker when I showcase how my content plays out in the business world and intertwines with the business life of specific audience members. It's as if they're getting their own personalized keynote. I'm using their names and making them feel like they're part of my content. Think of scenarios like this as win-win.

Another way to effectively use connections you have with individual members in any audience is to sing praises as you are in front of a larger group. I'll get into more detail about this in section IV. But for now, I'll share an example. My company, Roshini Multi Media, is a member of several chambers of commerce in the Minneapolis/St. Paul metro area. These chambers have monthly events for members and guests. If you're a business person, this probably sounds familiar. At many of these events, you get the chance to introduce yourself and say a line or two about what you do. I often try to compliment another member in my introduction when it's appropriate. Perhaps they're a new vendor of mine, and I want to highlight how they helped me through a computer nightmare. Perhaps they're a jeweler, and I want to point out how they helped me find the perfect gift. It doesn't take much time, but it's an easy addition to your own introduction that also solidifies your connection to them. Highlighting these connections in a short introduction also helps people who do not know you to think about starting a business relationship with you. After all, people like to do business with people they like and people they might already have a connection with through shared organization membership. When you can personalize even brief introductory moments and other business presentation moments within any of your business organizations, you benefit your bottom line.

REALIZE THERE ARE WILD CARDS

You can do your due diligence and ask all the necessary questions and still be left with one area to analyze and not overlook: *Realize there are wild cards in any audience.* Perhaps it's the know-it-all, or the cranky person, or the quiet one who won't engage when you call on her. Or maybe the wild card is the lone cowboy in this group of farmers. My best advice is to *not* let any wild card throw you. You've already figured out your intent for this group. And you are doing your audience analysis. The extent that you can know about and understand your wild card ahead of time, the better your chances of connecting with everyone in the audience. But realize you may only find out about the wild card audience member once you've launched into your presentation moment.

Learning of your wild card only after you've started your presentation moment brings you to the *during* part of your audience analysis.

The *during* is an area of audience analysis people rarely identify, or more importantly, often fail to prepare to face. The next chapter focuses on *during* audience analysis and offers some ideas for successful forays with wild cards and any additional new data you get about your audience once the performance begins.

TOOLBOX TALK

1. **Ask yourself *who* are the individuals in your group audience**
2. **Identify professions within thc group**
3. **Figure out commonalities among audience members**
4. **Be aware of any connections these audience members have to you**
5. **Prepare for wild cards**

CHAPTER 7

DURING THE PERFORMANCE

By now, I trust you've done your pre-show audience analysis. You have a clear sense of the makeup of the group with whom you'll share this presentation moment. You figured out whether certain members have any connections to you. You understand there might be a wild card or two in the audience. In general, you're feeling good about having prepared your content to cater to this particular audience. What could go wrong, right?

Well, another crucial part of Audience Analysis is keeping your eyes and ears open to analyzing the audience once you get to your presentation moment. I call this *during* analysis. *During* audience analysis need not be confusing. It's the phase that starts once you arrive at any in-person presentation and concludes at the end of the presentation moment itself or, if you are conducting a webinar or teleseminar, once you get started in the presentation moment. I want you to be prepared for what might happen if you begin your performance and realize something isn't quite as you planned or imagined based on your *before the show* analysis. You're going to be fine because I will give you some ways to sense if you are being well received or not. I give you tools for helping yourself as you help your audience understand your content. Here are a few things to keep in mind to help make sure you're as in tune with your audience as possible *during* performance.

GAUGE THEIR FEEDBACK

Your best indicator of who this audience is and its reaction to you once the performance begins is *this audience* and its visual or audible first reaction to you—eyes, body language, sometimes even silence. Try to gauge audience feedback. For instance, are they yawning, not laughing when they should, falling asleep, looking confused? This *during* audience analysis is really what separates the best communicators from the wannabes. But give yourself time. The *during* part of your audience analysis is likely the toughest audience analysis you'll face. If you can master this stage of audience analysis, however, you only have success ahead of you. Discomfort is normal with this stage of audience analysis. Even the pros don't always get it right when faced with a different audience from the one they expected. I'm not even sure all professional speakers take this level of audience analysis into account. Keep trying, and I guarantee you will be rewarded, whether that reward is more money by way of more speaking engagements, more satisfaction because of a job well done, or more visible smiles and nods from your audience because they're connecting with you and your content.

REACT TO INTERACTION

By now you probably know I'm an advocate of using interaction during your presentation moments. Fairly soon after you try an interactive moment with your audience, you should be able to decide if it's going over well. Be sure to respond to how your audience reacts to you during these interactive moments. Try to include interactive moments to help you understand your audience better. So your *during* performance audience analysis can take into account how audience members react to you when you interact with them. Do you see nods of agreement or understanding as your point is absorbed? Do they smile because they get the great analogy you just made?

If you see these positive reactions, react positively. Affirm your audience members. Call on someone if this is an appropriate place for an interactive moment. Sing (well, not literally) out a name and tell him you saw the light bulb light up for him. When you are able to react to interaction that's coming from your audience, you are observing and analyzing *during* your performance. This feedback, negative or positive, should help you fine-tune your content as you move forward both with this particular audience and with your presentation moments in general.

ADJUST TO THE CROWD

At this point, you've understood some of the feedback you're getting *during* performance. It may be negative; it may be positive. Either way, you are in a position to adjust to the crowd—giving your audience the best possible performance and not letting them down at the same time.

My big warning sign with adjustment is to not let it throw you. When you plan for the fact you may have to adjust, the less anxious you will be if adjustment becomes necessity. Remember you are adjusting in order to most successfully deliver your content to the audience that's in front of you. Take it as a gift if you get enough cues from your audience *during* performance that you realize you must adjust. Then do it.

Adjusting to the audience can take many forms. As you go through this process, you will develop your own methods. For now, some suggestions. First, perhaps you need to trim your topic. Trimming could require dropping some of the content and focusing on fewer key points. I helped one client with her keynote to an association of architects. She had so much knowledge and insight to share, the best advice I could give her was to edit. I knew if she trimmed her material, she'd be more effective in getting her big points out. Less really is more. And she followed up with me after her keynote to let me know she received exceptional feedback about how well the group took in her message.

Perhaps you need to help your audience understand one key point before you can move on to other parts of your overall presentation. Getting their full comprehension might require you to interact a little more, solicit their feedback, and look for recognition they're getting this key point before you bring in new material. I assume this isn't going to be a problem if you're someone who really knows your topic and can talk easily about any aspect of it at a moment's notice.

Adjustment may also take the form of changing the level of formality of your approach. For instance, let's say you're speaking in front of a group of financial planners. Well, a last-minute schedule adjustment (not in your control) was made to have you present at the end of a day-long golf tournament before the group headed to cocktail hour. Now you've got an adjustment to make for an audience about whom you had already done your *before the show* analysis. Audience moods may be different. The audience's setting and attire are even different. Now, they're in golf shirts and shorts and you're the only thing between them and their three-olive martinis. This shouldn't make you want to impress them less, but you do want to adjust to this crowd because their ability to take in your material is now directly affected by their new setting and attitude. So your *during* audience analysis and adjustment should reflect their needs.

You don't want to give up your desire to impress and convey information though. So figure out what you can drop, what you might need to add, ask yourself if you can now tell more jokes or adjust some of your content to reflect this more casual setting for this usually formal group. You likely will have to make these judgment calls on the spot. There might not be a lot of time to think and plan. Let the *before the show* audience analysis be one guide to audience traits that may help you make an honest and accurate assessment of the signs in front of you.

KEY IN ON CHARACTERS/WILD CARDS

You learned during your *before the show* analysis there may be wild cards in your audience. Those characters who may seem out of place. Perhaps they're cranky, quiet, or loners. One way to analyze your audience *during* performance is to locate these wild cards. Then decide if focusing on them will help increase your ability to connect with this entire audience. If you decide to *key in on wild cards*, you may be able to use these wild card audience members to focus how you adjust your content. Perhaps you can use the wild cards for interactive moments. Perhaps they will help you add humor to the presentation moment. For example, I gave a lunchtime keynote to a traditional business group that meets once a week. This civic organization raises money for the community, and its members help each other network. I realized *during* my performance there was a lot of camaraderie within this group. There was also a gentleman who sat with a table of all ladies and was good-naturedly teased during the introduction part of the luncheon event before I started my presentation. Of course, his fellow members were joking with him. But I decided to incorporate his status into my keynote as I realized he was quite a character in this group. At one point, I called on him for an exchange with me but called him by a fun nickname I made up that connoted someone who was good with the ladies. Everyone loved it—especially the character.

The good result for me was I took note of this character in my audience and didn't let him go to waste. Remember the *during* audience analysis starts when you arrive at your event. So I let myself mentally collect data even before my presentation itself started. I incorporated this man into my content to not only make a point but to have some fun with the entire audience. My favorite result was that you could see on his face he felt like a rock star. That kind of showcasing is always a bonus and something I purposely try to create whenever possible.

HOUSTON, WE HAVE A PROBLEM

I won't hide the fact you'll sometimes run into situations with your *during* analysis when you realize your presentation moment as planned won't fly. This can be very unsettling two minutes into a sixty-minute talk. Acceptance is the first step. You must now embrace the fact that Plan A has to go out the window. Yes, you must eject. Get yourself out of what you had planned and move into Plan B. That second plan may be something you have in your pocket, or it might be more on-the-spot. Just realizing the change-up scenario could happen to you actually starts to take some of the mystery out of surprise situations that may one day challenge you. And taking the mystery out of presentation by lowering the scary factor is all part of my goal. Knowledge is power and knowing that you may face the worst of all scenarios should actually be comforting because now you are starting to think about how to plan for this possibility.

If you have done thorough *before the show* audience analysis, you are now at an advantage. But even if you've planned for this scenario, it is usually unsettling. I can tell you that from experience. Therefore, remaining calm is your first step. We'll get into vocal exercises in the next section. But for now, I suggest you breathe. Breathe deeply and calmly. The simple act of breathing deeply helps the body to relax. Good body language at this stage will also give your voice and mind some time to recalibrate.

Now, get ready to showcase what you feel is important from this point on. It doesn't matter if your presentation moment shrinks in time. Shortening here will just give you more time at the end for a Question and Answer period. Showcase the key points of your content that you would deliver no matter how smoothly things might have gone. The difference is you realize your audience wasn't exactly what you expected, so you have to adjust how it comes out of your mouth now. You might have to add some interactive elements or drop them completely. Now is also when *less is more* comes into play big time. A common mistake of many presenters is they feel they have to jam a lot of content into little space. Let this about face in your presentation moment give you license to actually deliver fewer elements but deliver them more thoroughly for the audience you now find in front of you.

You will eventually take the data from your *during the performance* audience analysis and the results to help you with future presentation moments. I outline that in the next chapter dealing with *after the curtain call.*

TOOLBOX TALK

1. **Do not overlook instant feedback from your audience**
2. **React to your audience's interaction**
3. **Adjust to your crowd**
4. **Understand Plan A may go out the window; remain calm, and move into Plan B or beyond**

CHAPTER 8

AFTER THE CURTAIN CALL

Congratulations! By now, your presentation moment is wrapped. That's the good news. But your work is not complete. There is a third part to Audience Analysis that is crucial. I call it *after the curtain call.* The *after* audience analysis is important for the audience who just experienced you as well as for future audiences. Some might call this *after* analysis the follow-up.

However you choose to view it, making sure you incorporate this stage of audience analysis should ensure more success to come, whether that success comes in the form of more clients, more speaking gigs, or all around improvement as a communicator.

SOLICIT FEEDBACK IMMEDIATELY

When possible, try to get feedback directly from this audience to help you gauge how you did—what worked, what could use improvement. Some speakers leave evaluation forms for audience members to voluntarily fill out. When I am part of an audience and this happens to me, I tend to forget or disregard something that seems so cumbersome. But near the end of your presentation moment, you have an audience with whom you've developed some level of rapport. Now is your time to figure out a way to help them want to give you feedback and also make it easy for them to do so.

On the recommendation of one of my mentors in the speaking world, I started giving out small cards that ask just two questions. You can have these cards available prior to getting started and reference them at some point during your talk when you'd like your audience to focus on them. Or you can have an assistant or one of the event organizers pass them out as you are winding down your presentation moment. I tailored my questions on the small card to fit my business purposes, and you can do the same. For instance, the first question I ask: *Please share one thing Roshini discussed in this keynote that another colleague of yours would find beneficial.*

It's a pretty easy question, and it helps identify information the audience finds useful. With some presentation moments, I find that a majority of people write down the same answer in response to this question. That tells me a topic really hit home. It tells me there's a thirst for my particular delivery of this material. The feedback from my audience lets me know I need to keep that aspect of my content intact and even try to make it better. A second question I include often is focused at referrals: *What organization do you believe would benefit from a presentation by Roshini?*

I suggest you not ask more than two or three questions. The key is to get these postcards handed out when people are still in their seats anticipating the conclusion of your presentation. I often ask the host to pass them out. That way I can continue with my content and casually mention the cards and ask people to fill them out before they leave the room. Sometimes you'll get a 50 percent return rate. Sometimes you'll get closer to 100 percent. When you make it easy, chances are you'll get a better response than with other types of evaluation methods.

SOLICIT FEEDBACK OVER TIME

Another way to solicit feedback is to invite audience members to contact you with comments or questions. I assume by now audience members have material in front of them that includes your e-mail address, phone number, social media contacts, and Web site if you have one. This invitation also leaves the impression that you are open to ongoing dialog with your audience. This helps on multiple levels. If you would like to turn these people into future clients, you've opened the door to continued conversation.

If you want to be seen as a thought leader, you are putting audience members on notice that they can reach out to you. Why wouldn't they? You know your stuff. Perhaps you're even the expert. Whether you are a regular speaker or someone who dabbles in speaking engagements as a marketing tool, showcasing yourself and your unique perspective are key ways to build business. This is probably not news to you. But my goal is to help you understand how powerful presentation moments can establish, develop, and grow your ability to be seen as the expert.

YOUR GUT—THEIR REACTION TO YOU

Trust yourself as you reflect on the presentation moment and identify how you thought your audience reacted to you. Be honest and take note. This is a good place from which to design your follow-up methods. If you get the sense a group thank you is in order, send some notes or e-mails. If you heard one segment of your audience needs something in particular and you can be a resource, follow up with those people in particular. If you gathered their business cards at some point during your presentation moment, you should have no trouble contacting them. Your host or organizer is also a good reference. Build in a system of getting particular e-mail contact information for your audience when you agree to present for any particular organization.

There will be times your gut tells you the impression you left wasn't quite what you wanted or intended. I had an experience like that about a year after I started my company. It was a group of business people, mostly men but a lot of retirees. I was expecting few retirees and more than a majority of people currently in the work force. In retrospect, I probably hadn't done enough *before the show* audience analysis to prepare for that particular group. As I think back on that presentation moment and really listen to my gut, I've figured out many ways I could make the same presentation better if it were to happen today. An improved way of operating in the future, in itself, is a good result from doing some *after the curtain call* audience analysis. I've turned those bummer gut feelings into data I can use to improve in the future. Realize improved data is part of the goal with post-talk audience analysis. You are not giving presentation moments in a vacuum. Presentation moments should build on one another.

FOR FUTURE OR SIMILAR GROUPS

Part of the reason *after the curtain call* audience analysis is important is to take what you did well and what you could improve upon to future presentation moments. I'm amazed by the number of presenters who do not use the gold mine of current presentations to turn future ones into platinum.

Ask yourself a few questions as you reflect on your particular presentation moment. Will you speak to a group similar to this one anytime soon? Do you have a request to present this particular content in the near future? What really worked in this presentation? What could I make even better by fine-tuning a certain aspect of the presentation? For any presentation moment, you may come up with several questions. Or you may develop a permanent list of questions to ask yourself after you give every presentation.

The key is to make your *after the curtain call* audience analysis useful as you move forward. Collect the data, analyze it, and implement your findings.

TOOLBOX TALK

1. **Invite feedback directly from the audience—immediately**
2. **Solicit feedback over time—via e-mail, social media, telephone**
3. **Reflect on the job you did—write about it in your presentation journal**

CHAPTER 9

THEY'RE WITH YOU, NOT AGAINST YOU

One thing to remember at every level of Audience Analysis is: *They're With You, Not Against You.* When you give a presentation, big or small, your audience wants you to succeed. This sentiment should come as no surprise, but it's amazing how many people forget this truism during preparation and delivery of their presentation moments.

When you remember this, you put yourself in position for success. The first time I noticed the shock and awe of this concept was about a year after I started my business and gave a keynote called "Poise Under Pressure." When I talked about this idea, I saw a lot of heads nodding in agreement. But I also noticed many looks of surprise. People actually seemed to be hearing this concept for the first time. Try to keep your audience's good wishes in mind as you prepare for any presentation moment.

YOUR AUDIENCE WANTS YOU TO SUCCEED

Let's think about it in more detail with a clear head. You should realize your audience, whether one or one thousand, wants you to give them something. In other words, unless they're your main business competitor, they want you to succeed. Perhaps they're in the room to learn from your expertise. Perhaps the audience wants to be entertained or understand your sales offerings. Maybe this group hopes to get ideas to inspire their employees. My voice coach, Larry Russo, sums up the underlying sentiment: "People in front of you are spending their own precious time and attention to be part of your audience. If you do not succeed in giving them information or experience they find valuable, they have just wasted time and attention. Yup, your audience is always rooting for your success." They could have been doing something else during your presentation moment. Instead, these audience members are in front of you, either in-person or via webinar or teleseminar or some taped version of you, to gain something from your presentation moment. Embrace this concept, and you stay in position for success.

Perhaps you are speaking at a big corporate event. You need to realize, if you don't already know this, planners have spent several months to more than a year preparing. They are not going to put you on the program if they believe there's a strong likelihood you'll fail. At the very least, the event producer wants you to succeed. Take that as a word of comfort and a word of duty to them.

Be Gentle with Yourself

As you try to embody this concept of shared success with your audience, also remember to *be gentle with yourself.* Many times presenters put so much pressure on themselves to succeed, they forget to have fun and give themselves a break. This doesn't mean you're lazy or let yourself cut corners. But giving yourself the kind of respect and gentleness you'd bestow upon a friend or any member of your audience will help you stay calm and prepare, mentally and physically, in the most practical way.

YOUR AUDIENCE WANTS A QUALIFIED SPEAKER WHO KNOWS THE TOPIC

Underlying the idea of shared success is the assumption by your audience that you know what you're talking about. I'm a communication and media consultant; if I tried to pull off a talk about fishing, that wouldn't fly. That most likely would bring out skepticism from my audience. Self-perception and authenticity are key ingredients for successful delivery. No matter how much good energy my audience has for me, they're not impressed if I try to talk about something about which I'm not really qualified to speak. So when you try to deliver something you are less familiar with or that is a gray area for you, you set yourself up for failure. And I can see why presentation wouldn't be fun for you.

Event Planner Dana Ellis of Ellis International showcases reasons for going a step further and hiring a professional speaker over any other kind of speaker. "A pro is so familiar with what they're doing; they are better at answering questions. They give a good answer with a real world example," explains Ellis. You may not be at the level of professional speaker, and that's fine. But Ellis's comment underscores the importance of knowing your content and being prepared because the audience really does want someone who knows the topic and is qualified to teach others something.

Celebrate Your Accomplishment

I will assume you are giving presentation moments on your areas of expertise and you're seeking my insight to help you get to your WOW! Do remember celebration is an important part of creating your reality if you'd like to keep getting better. Celebration can mean different things to different people. For me, it includes dinner with a family member or fifteen minutes to break for a chai tea latte after my presentation. Sometimes you celebrate the big wins, and other times you pat yourself on the back for the seemingly small milestones. For example, perhaps you tailored one of your anecdotes to a particular audience, and it really hit home with them. Celebrate! That may seem like a minor accomplishment to you, but it shouldn't. Remember: Connecting with an audience in a direct way is no small feat. Conversely, soak it up when you know you've made a major step on the road to your WOW! You have obvious reason for accolades. Be gentle with yourself and be your own cheerleader.

Celebration also serves another purpose. In celebration, you reflect. And when you reflect, you figure out more ways to fine-tune your skills and become more in-tune with your audience. I'm always going to suggest you self-analyze. Taking reflection a few steps further to self-analysis is healthy and productive. Self-analysis also helps you be more efficient during future preparation. Collect the data, use it, and do remember to celebrate all your milestones.

One favorite story for me was with a group of media consulting clients. The person who brought me in was going to get trained along with a few of her colleagues. Through my own audience analysis of this group ahead of time (the *before* audience analysis) and once the first session got started (the *during*), I knew I had a tough crowd. But I continued with what I had planned because I knew I had great material to offer and share. I tried not to forget this group wanted me to succeed, even if a couple of them weren't the most smiley. When the three-hour first session wrapped, I got a chance to debrief with the person who brought me in. She was so pleased with how the session went. She shared with me that she had been worried for me in front of this group of multiple, intense personalities. She told me she realized within a few minutes that I had impressed her colleagues and they were slowly opening themselves up to really learning. She knew them well and could gather that without much analysis and certainly more quickly than I could at that point.

But had I panicked at the moment I realized this could be a tough bunch of nuts to crack, I would have been less than successful. Instead, I kept focused on my intent for this particular audience, and I remembered *they wanted me to succeed.* And over time, I continued to work with this group plus some additional colleagues of theirs. To this day, the group is among my favorite clients. The fact that each individual in that group has had some follow-up consulting with me and continues to call on me for media insight and presentation expertise also showcases their belief in my qualifications. Repeat business is one of the best compliments. And it helps me stay energized to continue to come up with new and creative ways to help this client group grow as communicators.

By now you should have focused direction for a thorough understanding of *who* will be in front of you. But all could be lost if you don't deliver your material to your particular audience in a way that best suits its particular personality.

In section III, I help you stay focused with your I-A-P™ Formula and identify key tools for a powerful performance.

TOOLBOX TALK

1. Expect good vibes and positive energy from your audience
2. Be gentle with yourself; give yourself a break when appropriate
3. Breathe
4. Celebrate successful presentation moments

SECTION III

POWERFUL PERFORMANCE

Look Mom, It's Me

CHAPTER 10

TECHNICAL DETAILS

Clients often hear me say, "It doesn't really matter what you *know*, if you don't know how to *present* it." There's a reason for these words. Think about people who are memorable to you. Do you remember them because of their titles or for the knowledge in their brains? Or do you remember them because of the way they told you about what they knew and delivered their content well? Chances are the latter. Powerful performance encompasses a fine-tuned delivery of your content. You use your face, your body, and your vocal behavior to get to your WOW! Before you can deliver well, you must have a setting that supports your intent and helps you present your best. You must take charge of the *technical details*.

OH, WHAT A LOVELY ROOM

Let's say you are giving a keynote to three hundred people next month. Not a bad gig, but one that presents different challenges compared with speaking to three people in a conference room. You are going to face two different options when it comes to the setting of your presentation moment. Either you choose the venue or someone chooses it for you. You generally have a lot more control when you can choose the setting.

Your physical setting includes the room you're in and the arrangement of that room. Sometimes I'm asked how I want tables arranged. If given the option, I always answer with my preference and don't leave room arrangement to chance or to someone else's choice. Ask yourself how you can help make the setting more conducive to a positive and successful presentation moment. These seemingly small details can make a world of difference. If you want to know about optimal room aesthetics, take note of these instructions.

First, you want to make sure everyone can see you. If it's a large audience, that goal may require technology. If it's a webinar, you want to make sure the picture quality of the screen doesn't include strange lines or lighting. In either the in-person or webcast scenario, you may be projected onto big screens in various parts of the space your audience views you. One annual event I attended showcased the action on large screens around the auditorium. It included a brown background on stage. That was also the background behind the speakers as they got up to deliver various parts of the program. Several of these presenters also wore brown, so they blended into their background. On the big screen, this looked silly. This scenario could have easily been avoided. But room control requests require assertiveness from you. Ask what the colors of the room are; by this, I mean the actual colors of the walls and any accessories that might be in the room. Ask about staging. Even better, try to visit the space ahead of time to see for yourself.

If you intend to be interactive, as I hope you will be, you also want to figure out if the room itself provides space for you to move around. If your audience is smaller and confined to a conference room setting, you need to figure out if you're comfortable moving around in that space. If they're all sitting in close proximity to you and to each other, it may seem strange for you to be standing the entire time. You may want to sit. Or you may decide you'll sit for part of the presentation and stand for other parts. It just depends on the layout of the room and your intent as a presenter. The more you know about what's available to you, the better equipped you are to decide. And as you analyze the space, do not sacrifice good sound quality or the ability for the audience to clearly see what you want them to see. I've given presentations in conference rooms where there's one long table with five to fifteen people seated facing one another. At one table like that, I might choose to sit more of the time and stand some of the time. However, I've also been in the same size conference room with several tables of two or three people a piece. They're all facing the front as opposed to one another. In that case, I probably would stand more, so everyone could see. If I feel varying up my positioning would help delivery, I may sit during parts of the presentation.

You can answer many of these spatial questions and get a sense of what's best for your particular situation by visiting your venue prior to your presentation moment. There are times when a site visit is not possible due to your schedule, the venue's schedule, or distance challenges. But to the extent you can, make time for a site visit as part of your preparation; it will help you relax and become more focused for this particular audience. You will be that much more in control of the pacing and structure of your talk because you worked through space usage, venue challenges, and positive aspects of the room as part of the big picture in getting to your WOW!

In the case where you cannot pre-visit your space, here are some key questions for which you should get answers prior to getting to your venue. The meeting planner is the likely person to ask:

- *Do you have a Web site that would allow me to have a virtual tour of the space where I will present?*
- *What other associations or organizations have spoken at your venue?*
- *Is there a meeting planner assigned to my event and/or me?*
- *Who is the audio visual professional assigned to my room at this event?*
- *What's the physical makeup of the room in which I'll present; is it hooked up for any technical equipment I'll need/bring?*

I have a client I prepped to moderate a big industry event in Las Vegas. During his preparation, we talked through how many people would be on stage and how we could arrange their seating. I asked him if he'd have a chance to visit the exact venue prior to his morning plenary session. He said he and the five people on the panel would meet in the exact room the evening prior. Great! I advised him—as the event moderator—to tell everyone at the pre-show meeting where they would sit on stage. I also suggested he use the site visit to get a sense of how he'd work the stage the next day during his presentation moment. In case you're wondering, he text messaged me immediately after his plenary with excitement about his success.

Other factors to assess during any site visit include: temperature;

proximity of the stage (if there is a stage) to the audience; ability to roam around if you do not plan to stay planted; sounds or noises coming from the door, hallway, or adjacent rooms when the door is both opened or closed; and,very importantly, lighting.

LIGHT CHECK

You've probably seen it happen. No matter how high-tech function halls become, it happens. You came to hear and see a speaker, but you can't really see the speaker. The speaker may be backlit because the event planner put him or her in front of a large window. You know the scenario; it's almost painful to look because you're staring into bright sunlight. And if you're staring into light, that means your light is behind the speaker instead of on the speaker's face. No one bothered to analyze the space before setting up for the speaker. So you can't see your speaker well either. Or perhaps you can't see your speaker's face because the darkest area of the venue was selected for this presentation, and no one thought about much-needed lighting.

I want you to be the person who does think about lighting when you are preparing for a presentation moment. Good lighting should make you look like a movie star and not a shadow in a horror movie. The light source should be in front of what needs to be lit and not behind the subject. In a close-knit setting, ideally the light source is a little off to the side in front of the presenter. In a large function area, things may vary. There may be spotlights and all-over-room lights. As long as you, the presenter, are clearly visible, and the lighting is flattering, you will be in good shape. Keep in mind a light bulb may blow at the last minute. Make sure you know how to call maintenance when you need someone immediately.

CAN YOU HEAR ME?

Another bummer—when you can't hear the presenter.

Ask AV Person to Stick Around

Audio snafus are so avoidable, it makes me cringe every time I witness them. The audio issue is also one you should take charge of ahead of time. Perhaps it's because of my past life as a TV news reporter in a world where sound issues are just as important as visual ones that audio is a particular focus area for me. Imagine if you were watching your favorite news anchor on CNN or Fox News, and you couldn't hear him or her? Maybe you've even seen this happen. Most people change channels until they find someone they can hear. That live report of the latest Florida hurricane would seem a lot less vivid with no sound, right? Imagine the presentation you've worked so hard to deliver, and one or more people in your audience cannot hear you—not a winning situation for anyone.

Your site visit to the venue is your opportunity to look into what you'll face when it comes to being heard, literally. Secondly, the twenty to sixty minutes prior to your presentation moment, if you have the luxury of that option, is your final opportunity to get some help from an audio pro and ensure you'll be heard. Ask the sound person to stick around. He or she shouldn't mind and would rather have a successful audio experience than a disaster or having to be called back in front of the audience to fix the audio. Sometimes you'll be in a venue in which the sound person already checked your microphone and says it's ready to go. I suggest you check it with the sound person present. Sound check your own voice and make sure everything's working with the audio equipment. Make sure the sound level settings are not too soft or too loud. You don't want to blow anyone out of the venue, but you also don't want to be so soft people are straining to hear you.

Microphone Do's and Don'ts

And that brings me to the focal point of quality sound—the microphone. You may have one or several in use during your presentation moment. The microphone needs to be checked well in advance of when you'll use it with your audience. If you're in a teleseminar or webinar setting, you may not even be in the same space, let alone city, as your sound technicians. Give yourself plenty of time to do these sound checks prior to presenting. And reserve that twenty to sixty minutes before you actually present for final checks. Perhaps you're in a time crunch. At the very least, have someone on your team sound check everything with the audio pros. But realize there's no substitute to you doing this yourself with your own voice. There are good microphones and not-so-hot ones. And everyone's voice has a different relationship with various mics. Remember this is *your* presentation moment. Your name is on the program or up in lights. Don't you want to be the one to make sure you sound great? And remember expectations—yours, the audience's, and the host's—you have a responsibility to fulfill.

Getting your technical details in order before your audience arrives is a key part of successful presentation moments. The more you know about a room, its lighting, and audio strengths and challenges of any space, the more likely you are to WOW!

Now, it's time to focus on you.

TOOLBOX TALK

1. **Preview your presentation space and the physical arrangement within that space**
2. **Make sure your lighting flatters you and your performance**
3. **Confirm your sound equipment works for your presentation style**
4. **Check microphone(s) in advance of the start of your performance**
5. **Ask venue's audio visual person to stick around at the beginning of your performance**

CHAPTER 11

IMAGE

If you're making the effort to make sure *how* you're technically seen and heard are in order, you might as well make sure *who* your audience sees is also top-notch. There can be no powerful performance without a strong *image*. Image includes your face, hair, and clothing. But for the bigger picture, I'd like you to think of your image work as building your personal presence—your style.

FIRST IMPRESSION

You have probably heard this statistic: First impressions are made within ten seconds of someone meeting you. For the performer, the first impression can be extended to someone seeing you in-person, watching you on a screen, and/or hearing only your voice. Without trying to make you overly self-conscious, I do want you to realize the effort you put into making a strong first impression will also help with how your entire presentation moment goes. Remember back to the Intent stage of the I-A-P™ Formula? A powerful performance helps you carry out your intent for this presentation moment. And your intent helps guide how you prepare to perform powerfully. Each part of the formula is co-equal. So the work you put into defining your intent will serve you well at the Powerful Performance stage.

People tend to consciously and subconsciously read the vibe you give. Much of your vibe has to do with what people see. Think about it. You make the same judgments when you meet someone in a social setting, in a business setting, or before you watch someone give a presentation of any kind. Do you ever stop to ask yourself what kind of personal presence you emit? Do you ask for regular feedback from your colleagues and peers about what their first impressions of you tend to be?

You can gain some insight from casually asking around—ask people who will be honest with you. We don't always know the kind of first impression we put out there unless we do a little data gathering and analysis of how people receive us. The most powerful performers have a keen sense of their image, their style, their vibe. They're not copying anyone else, and they learn how to maintain their top form even when they find themselves a little under the weather.

A FACE THAT ONLY A MOTHER COULD LOVE

Your face is a valuable communication asset. Most people do not realize the extent to which a face is a communication tool. First do a quick facial analysis of yourself. This includes whether or not you think your face is pleasing to look at or whether it has some unusual or distinctive feature. But on another level, really try to understand what your best facial features are and learn how to use them as tools for powerful communication. One image exercise I do with my clients is to have them define their best facial feature. If you believe X is your best facial feature, you are in position to consider that feature a communication asset. Let me describe and analyze a few of the main communication assets on your face.

Eyes

The eyes absolutely have it. They can be your best friend or your worst enemy. You might hear people compliment your beautiful or expressive eyes. Do you ever ask yourself *how* you're using them? If your eyes are an obvious asset from an aesthetic or visual standpoint, start to think about what they're doing during presentation moments. Are they smiling, laughing, or frowning? No matter what they're doing, your eyes are either helping you be a more powerful performer, or they're hindering your ability to connect with your audience.

Let's say you have fantastic eyes that are quite expressive. You may have to tone them down if you have a topic that is sensitive. If *not* giving something away with the use of your eyes is crucial, then you must be conscious of what your eyes are doing and whether or not you're giving off negative feelings by using your eyes in a certain way.

On the flip side, if you have a joyous topic, and your eyes are subdued and negative, you won't be effective either.

The important thing is to understand how you're using your eyes and try to use them in a way that enhances your presentation moment. One way to do that is to intentionally communicate with your eyes. Use solid eye contact with your audience. I don't want you to get into any stare-downs with anyone. But really look into people's eyes. I suggest you do not look over their heads at different points in the room. Even if you're on a screen and not directly in front of a live audience, good eye contact with the camera means you're looking directly into your viewers' eyes. You've seen the opposite, haven't you? That's when the person is on screen, and he's looking down or off to the side. That's off-putting and actually makes the presenter seem shady. A TV consultant once told me when I was in TV news, "You kiss your boyfriend with your mouth and your viewers with your eyes." That comment really stuck with me because it was a symbol of the bigger message: Your eyes speak volumes—whether your mouth's involved or not.

Mouth

Another important facial feature is your mouth, and connected to that, your smile. I ask my presentation clients if they smile easily. The main reason I ask this is to figure out how much effort it will be for them to just relax and let their senses of humor or affability shine through. Some people are more comfortable with this than others. Your ability to naturally smile also connects with your ability to be authentic. I notice many people turn into a formal or rigid version of themselves during presentation moments. This is the last thing you want when you're trying to deliver a powerful performance. That rigidity hurts your ability to smile naturally, seem approachable to your audience, and put your audience at ease.

There are going to be times when too much smiling will be unnatural and, frankly, unwanted. For example, doing a television live shot at a murder scene was not the time to be flashing my big smile. Not every presentation setting or topic will be that obvious, however. By having your intent nailed down and your audience analyzed before you're at your presentation moment, you should have the information you need to assess what's required of you as a presenter. It's important you do the assessment you need to do ahead of time. Once you determine your facial communication assets, you can start shifting into using them as powerful communication tools.

Jaw Line and Bone Structure

Sometimes clients tell me their strong jaw line or great bone structure is their facial asset. I say great! You're blessed with good genes as well as a facial feature that lends itself to credibility. Strong bone structure is associated with credible people. Think military types, pilots, CEOs. Right or wrong, that's the association. Now, the jaw line or great bone structure is your asset to run with or not use well. Because depending on whatever else is going on with your face, strong bone structure can add to beauty or give a sinister or rigid impression when not used well. You can make that determination yourself from your own analysis as well as what other people tell you about their reaction to your face. And by this, I mean their reaction to your face when you are speaking *and* when you're not speaking.

Once you've made the determination, you can play up the strong bone structure or play it down. Playing it up or down may involve the use of other facial features as well as the use of your body. I'll get more into body movement later in chapter thirteen. For now, I'll touch on a couple concepts. You can use your eyes and mouth naturally and to their best potential to help bring out your strong facial bone structure. When your audience sees you using the other assets well, they'll naturally be in a positive frame of mind to think about whatever aspects of your image they like. And if your audience is reacting to what they see on your face—from your eyes, to your smile, to your solid jaw line—they are receiving a good performance. I hope it's a powerful performance. Think of good facial bone structure as the foundation for a strong face—the foundation for a face that's just waiting to perform powerfully.

HAIR: YOU WEAR IT EVERY DAY

Do you know what a good hair day is? If you're like many people, you know when you're having one but might not know how to describe it. And somehow it kind of makes everything else better.

To help my journalism students figure out their good hair day definition plus make their hair more in their control, I called on the experts. Master Colorist William Anderson of Salon Lili in Minneapolis came to the University of Minnesota to conduct an image workshop with the young men and women in my class. He brought a hair stylist with him to share tips. As several students got their mini-consults, I witnessed some transformations. My students probably didn't even notice on how many levels their enthusiasm for this newfound understanding shined.

The hair pros got my students to internalize how important the right hair is for anyone's overall look. For these future journalists, equating professional and polished appearance with credibility hit home.

Sure, students got some *subtle* basic tips such as, "Those sideburns are turning into pork chops." Or, "Perhaps that shade of red isn't naturally found on earth." But these image experts showed, by example, how they change lives daily. What a remarkable reward!

Whether you need to grow it out or cut it, color it or let your natural hue come back, may you remember something one of my former TV news anchors told me when I worked in TV news in Minneapolis: "Your hair is something you wear every day." So why not treat it as well or better than a favorite suit?

The Hairy Hybrid—Facial Hair

Less is more truly rules when it comes to facial hair. In general, facial hair is out. I do not hide the fact that I am not in favor of mustaches on men (or women for that matter), and it is a rare gentleman who looks good in a mustache. If you are one of those men for whom a mustache looks good and is part of your authentic style, great. For most men, however, a solo mustache makes you look outdated and unkempt. I cannot endorse it for powerful presentation.

My only caveat is the well-kept goatee. This only works, though, if you have a face for a goatee. Your stylist or barber should be able to give you some honest answers in that department. For certain thin faces, a goatee can add fullness and even credibility or polish. Again, ask your friends and family. Send me a photo. You should know by now I won't hold back my true feelings on this hairy issue. I will definitely say yes to your facial hair if it enhances your face and could help your overall look.

Remember, any facial hair is part of your image. So if you do look good in a beard and it helps you feel confident, keep it trimmed and clean. Your face helps you communicate not only your message, but also *who* you are. If you're a financial planner who wants to get prospects to invest their life savings with you, think about how a few days of whisker growth affects your credibility. If you look like you can't take care of yourself, why should I think you would take care of my money?

If you're a social media guru marketing how forward thinking and progressive you are, wearing a bushy mustache gives us a flashback to a time we may not want to return style-wise. There's a contradiction between how you want others to receive and perceive you and what your image is telling them. I want you, the presenter, to think about the various elements that go into powerful performance. When you understand how one no-shower day or letting that haircut go a couple weeks too long can affect your bottom line, I hope you have a newfound understanding of the importance of image to your bigger business goals and, frankly, your bottom line.

CLOTHING: WHAT DECADE ARE YOU LIVING IN?

To some, clothing is a source of great joy and a chance to show off personality. To others, it's a nuisance they must put up with so they're not walking around in the buff. To the presenter, realize your clothing is part of your communication toolbox. Your wardrobe helps deliver your credibility and ultimately your message. I do not want you to obsess about it, but I do want you to think about your clothing choices. And in some cases, you may need to do some overhauling.

Know Yourself and Dress Accordingly

If you're a cowboy, you probably won't feel comfortable in an Armani suit. If you're a banker, you probably know you can't walk into a client meeting without a tie. Your style is a combination of factors. Your style is what you're comfortable in plus what is required of you in your role as a business person. There are going to be clothes I might wear in my truly social and personal time that I wouldn't walk on stage in to give a keynote. That's just fine. The main point is to understand what you want to wear and what's required of you. For some, those two clothing personalities collide. So how do you reconcile?

As a communication consultant, I will always want you to err on the side of being over-dressed rather than under-dressed. You want to make sure you never insult your audience by your choice of clothing. *Less is more* can also guide you. If you're uncomfortable wearing trend items, stick with the basics. Fill your closet with classic pieces that won't quickly go out of date. This goes for men and women. If you like fad, have some classic black, gray, and blue in your closet. Then, make a spark by having accent pieces in the hot colors of the season. Some years orange is in, and other years orange really should only be seen on pumpkins.

Flatter Yourself

On your own or with the help of a personal shopper or stylist, it's also a good idea to know which colors look good on you. Get a sense of colors you know you look good in and ones you know you love to wear. Those lists may or may not be the same. But they should turn out to be a good assortment of colors you feel authentically powerful wearing. For men, pick up some unusual ties. Or go for a dapper colored vest underneath the sport jacket. I'm a big fan of royal purple and red. Both are power colors. For men, a great solid or patterned royal purple tie with an ice purple (almost-not-there purple, but not quite white) is one good combination. For women, a jacket or big-collared blouse in a red or royal purple makes a statement. Know yourself and find these pop colors in items authentic to you. I also challenge you to go a bit outside your comfort zone in search of WOW!'s you may not even realize you can pull off.

I always ask my clients what suit style looks best on them. Once I get their answer, I then determine if that's a suit style that is current and flattering for their shape, style, and occupation. If you are going to have a power suit, it should be one that's universally recognized as flattering and polished.

Adjust to Your Audience

For any given presentation moment, having done a good audience analysis will also help guide you with wardrobe. If you know you're presenting to a bunch of accountants, you'd normally assume pretty conservative dress. But after doing your pre-show audience analysis, you may find out you will present at the group's annual golf outing. Everyone will be in casual wear. I hope you adjust. You don't want to dress ultra informally, but you also don't want to be the only one in a suit. Figure out what works with that setting for that audience within your style parameters. Always ask your host for clarification about the audience and setting for optimum wardrobe results.

Look the Part

I cannot stress enough how important it is for you to look like the professional you hold yourself out to be. I'm a presentation consultant. If I were to walk into my next client meeting wearing my favorite cargo pants and a little hoodie, I'd probably be laughed out of the room. As well I should be.

Also figure out if you need to be aware of any technology as you figure out your wardrobe. If you're going to be on a screen, there are certain patterns you should avoid. You'll get a sense of this with practice. But in general, solid colors are best. I suggest you don't go too light or too dark. The blue family is always good for on-screen. Unless you're being taped on a blue screen. Then avoid blue entirely to avoid blending into your background.

My goal for you is two-fold when it comes to your overall image—stay authentic and go for stylish credibility. You are being judged, graded, or analyzed before you even open your mouth. If your face, hair, and wardrobe are authentic and polished, you position yourself for the WOW! once you do open your mouth to speak.

TOOLBOX TALK

1. **A great presentation moment always starts with positive self-perception**
2. **Your face, hair, and wardrobe convey messages**
3. **Know your facial communication tools and use them**

   –Some examples: eyes, mouth, jaw line, bone structure
4. **Remain authentic but aim for style and polish with your clothing/accessories**

CHAPTER 12

VOCAL BEHAVIOR

The ultimate goal for the business presenter is to be seen as an authority on a given subject. Whether your intent is to entertain or to get everyone in the room to go green at corporate headquarters or to pledge $1,000 to your non-profit, you likely want people to view you as someone who has an authoritative grasp on your topic. Most people don't bother spending time to take in any kind of presentation unless they believe the person who's speaking has material to share from a position that's going to enlighten.

One of your most powerful tools for being seen as that authority is your own vocal behavior. I am not just talking about your voice. I will break down those details as we move along. Your voice plays a big role in how vocal behavior is experienced by your receiver, but your voice is not the sole player when it comes to this key component for communication success. Visualize vocal behavior as consisting of three components:

1. *How you sound*
2. *How you deliver your sound*
3. *How people receive your sound*

HOW YOU SOUND

When I talk about sound, I'm referring to the **quality** and **personality** of your voice. Is it loud, soft, nasal, gruff, or some sort of combination of a number of characteristics? The sound of your voice also includes your **pitch** and **tone**. Is your pitch in a deep part of your vocal register or is it in the higher end? Does the tone of your voice seem friendly or condescending? (See Vocal Behavior Evaluation in Appendix B, page 133; answer the questions there before you move on.)

Some people have distinct-sounding voices. Lauren Bacall, for instance, will be remembered as much for her acting as for her deep voice. James Earl Jones characterized the now iconic role of Darth Vader in the movie *Star Wars* by using the alpha male sound of his voice. Those deep and powerful sounds coming out of the black-masked caped Vader contribute to helping us visualize someone with a dominant personality—in essence, a strong vocal behavior. We can't really look at a photo of Darth Vader and *not* call to mind, or ear, Jones's rich and deep voice. In fact, if we saw the character of Darth Vader on the screen and heard a fragile voice come out of his mask, it would not compute. The vocal behavior of Darth Vader is distinct and got its signature from the rich personality and deep quality of James Earl Jones's voice. That vocal behavior made Darth Vader believable as a serious force and ruthless villain.

The sound of someone's voice can also be an impediment to his or her most powerful vocal behavior. For instance, have you ever heard a female executive open her mouth and sound like a little girl? Men and women can sound as if they have a child trapped in an adult's body. Most people don't realize that with some work, this obstacle can be minimized or overcome. The majority of us have spoken voices with two octaves worth of notes. That's sixteen notes your voice box is capable of producing. Your spoken voice is actually controlled by a different half of your brain than your singing voice. So when I talk about notes, I am referring to your spoken voice and not your singing voice. In my case it's easy to stick with the spoken voice because there's not much of a singing voice. I mention the difference because if you are a singer, you need to focus on your spoken voice and away from your singing voice. Do not be discouraged if you have a beautiful singing voice but feel your spoken voice isn't powerful. You are here to work on strengthening your spoken voice.

Pitch is another aspect of your sound. Your best pitch equals the best note on your spoken voice scale. Your *best* note should be natural to you, but it should also be the note that sounds the richest and most authoritative. I will introduce you to some vocal exercises later in this section to help you find your pitch. For now, take a moment to read the preceding paragraph out loud. Listen to yourself while you read out loud. Where on your vocal scale do you think your pitch falls?

Does it sound like it's too high, too low, or just right? Even better, tape record yourself reading the preceding paragraph out loud. The best pitch for you will not sound fake, but it will showcase someone who is an authority in your field and exudes confidence.

And then there's *tone*, which I'll loosely describe as your voice's personality. Does your voice say approachable, angry, condescending. You get the picture. If you had to think of one word someone might use to describe you just by hearing your voice, you're getting at tone. I assure you as we talk about vocal health and vocal exercises, you will start to feel the sounds.

For now, I want you to wrap your brain around why sound, pitch, and tone taken together can land you in a positive place or a negative one. Rocky Balboa from the *Rocky* movies is a less-authoritative, though friendly, sounding male character than, say, Dirty Harry. Part of why you make that determination consciously or subconsciously is because of the vocal behavior of those characters. Singer Annie Lennox has a rich and deep female voice. Whereas Dolly Parton's voice is more girly-girl or feminine. They both are successful singers but showcase different vocal behavior. Therefore, we associate different traits with each of them. If you're familiar with religious pesonalities, imagine what Moses or Mohammad or even the Hindu goddess Laksmi would sound like. Do you think their voices were wimpy? I think we all believe they had rich powerful voices that made them leaders and people others wanted to follow. It all starts with your vocal behavior. You can't do much unless people you want to buy from you, elect you, or follow you down the Nile believe you are what you hold yourself out to be. Weak voices rarely get powerful results.

HOW YOU DELIVER YOUR SOUND

I identified a few strong voices that exhibit positive vocal behavior to showcase how good it can get when your sound is strong. But what if you're someone who isn't quite at the vocal power level of Lauren Bacall or James Earl Jones? Or, what if you're in the ballpark, but you don't really know how to get to your WOW!? Well, my friend, there is hope. How you *deliver* your sound is more in your control than you think. Taking care of your larynx—the voice box—is the first step. And with a little focus, you can find your best sound.

Vocal Health

Let's talk a little bit about vocal health. As I write this sentence, I'm accompanied by one of my favorite things, a chai tea latté. This is one of the greatest drinks on earth. It has dairy in it, though, which can be an enemy of powerful performance. The very fact that I'm drinking it right now means I don't have an important presentation moment in the next few hours.

Dairy is one of the categories of food and drink that clogs the larynx. And a clogged larynx can't be there for you when you need to perform. You're generally safe if you avoid dairy products of any kind three hours prior to a presentation moment. But I advise even more caution—simply avoid all dairy the day of any presentation moment or the night before any morning presentation. Even if that means going hours without your double latté with a shot of espresso or banana split after your daughter's piano recital.

Before I go on, I will mention I don't claim to be a nutritionist or a medical expert. I share food and drink comments as they relate to vocal health. My advice comes from experiencing how various food and drink items affected my own performance during years of professional speaking and broadcasting. When you intentionally take notice of vocal health, you get highly in touch with what works and what hurts when it comes to hydration, nutrition, and powerful performance. Staying aware and using your own data collection in the area of vocal health will help you perform more powerfully every time you open your mouth. Data collection can happen in many ways but should always involve paying attention to what you eat and drink. Then record how it affects your overall performance. I assign my clients the presentation journal. I will give you detailed instruction on the presentation journal in the next chapter. For now, think about how best you can get yourself to record reflections about your presentation moments. Is it with a computer file, a notebook next to your bed, or a journal you keep at the office?

We take for granted how easy it can be for tastes of certain seasons to get in the way of our vocal health. Summer, for instance, brings higher sweet tooth craving levels and easier access to ice cream cones and frozen alcoholic concoctions. Sodas go down fast, and margaritas tend to flow. Enjoy! But remember timing with your imbibing. Drink lots of water to stay hydrated in preparation for presentation moments and interviews. Avoid sugary drinks before you present. Stay away from dairy before that big keynote, sales meeting, or afternoon of prospecting phone calls. Caffeine presents a unique situation. For some, it's to be avoided. I for one, cannot and do not drink it prior to performance—mainly because I'm a high-energy person, and caffeine would only make me appear frenzied. If you are someone who needs your morning coffee just to wake up, avoiding it could be detrimental to your presentation moment. The best advice is to experiment with caffeine and take notes about how it affects you. Then, proceed accordingly.

Vocal Exercises

A key way to work on your overall performance is to take some time for vocal exercises. The larynx is an instrument. And just like any instrument, it needs practice and maintenance. One of my favorite things to teach and do with clients is vocal exercises. I thank my voice coach, Larry Russo, for getting me on that road a few months before I started my television news career many years ago. I wasn't always as diligent with my own exercises at first. But as I did them, felt them, and saw results, I knew Larry was right.

For purposes of this book and in line with my mission to keep things simple for you, the reader, I'd like to keep these exercises low-key. I want you to actually do them. So we'll start with the basics. You can take the ones you learn here and do them more often, or for a longer duration, and build on what you started. You are in the driver's seat with vocal exercises. If you do them regularly, you will see results. Initially, the results may seem minor. But over time and with regular practice, many people experience major results. Those results can include moving your natural speaking voice to its most authoritative and resonant note. In my case, major changes took years; minor changes sometimes weeks. But with faithful repetition, these vocal exercises can help you become a more powerful performer.

The Yawn

You're probably saying: What is she talking about? Yawning's an exercise? But it's so easy. You're right; this is your warm-up, and it's not difficult. I told you I would keep things simple. You can do this. Here are my few tips for turning something you do every day into your most basic vocal exercise.

Form: First, stand up. If you must sit, fine. But standing is preferred. Second, open your mouth wide. Don't cover your mouth. Don't hold back. This is a vocal exercise. You have nothing to be embarrassed about—no one's watching unless you want them to. Third, let your arms move around should your yawning cause movement. Fourth, don't be afraid to fake big yawns or make noises with your yawns. You'll get more out of them because this will lead to more real yawns.

Benefits: The yawn relaxes the voice box. The yawn cools the brain, which might be overheating as it subconsciously realizes you have a presentation moment coming up. Or it might be heating up if you're just having a busy day and have lots to mentally juggle.

The Hiss

The second exercise in your routine is The Hiss. One of my clients likes this one so much he's replaced previous, shall we say unwanted, physical gestures at other drivers when he feels road rage. He now hisses at those drivers. He gets in his vocal exercises, and he doesn't get run off the road for finger obscenities.

Form: Continue to stand and plant your feet about shoulder width apart. First, fill your lungs with air from your diaphragm. Second, formulate your mouth as if you're about to hiss. Third, let out a loud hiss noise and visualize yourself sending the hiss across the room. Lastly, try to make that hiss loud and long. That means work on exerting some breath control without petering out too fast. Over time with practice, your hiss will sound louder and last longer.

Benefits: The hiss builds lung capacity. The hiss helps with projection. If you lose strength in your voice as the day goes on, the hiss is a great exercise to help you build energy into those muscles and your lungs.

The Ah-Scale

Remember I mentioned pitch? The Ah-Scale will help you find your pitch. In fact, it will help you find all the notes you are capable of creating with your larynx. With this vocal exercise, you will be making quite a bit more noise than with the hiss. Be sure to find a place where you feel comfortable doing so. By way of preparation, visualize yourself starting at your highest spoken note and try to find, or place, note after note as you move down the scale of your spoken voice. Visualize a flute player going down a scale according to her sheet music.

Form: First, stand with your feet planted and shoulder width apart. Second, relax your shoulders. You will be starting at your highest note and ending on your lowest note. Again, you have the ability to make sixteen notes worth of sound. I don't expect you to do that the first time around. But it is something to work toward. Each note will come out of your mouth and should last two to four seconds. You then move on and find the next note down the scale. Each note gets its own breath. So you do not have to try all your notes on one load of air.

Now third, open your mouth wide and keep your chin level. Ready? Project your first AH-sound. You are literally saying ahhhhh each time. End that note and move on to the next AH. Keep on going down the scale until you get really low and probably gravelly at the bottom of your scale. Be sure to keep your mouth open wide, project, and visualize subtle changes from note to note.

Benefits: The Ah-Scale helps you locate all the notes of your spoken voice. Once you find them, you can start to identify which one you normally speak with on a regular basis. When you identify your personal pitch placement, you can then figure out if it's the strongest note you are capable of using.

If it is your strongest note, great. Continue to use your new vocal exercises to empower your strong note. If it is *not* your strongest note, you have now heard some of your other notes. Can you identify one of those notes as a stronger pitch placement for your voice? Once you identify it, practice using it in speech. You might try to record yourself speaking or reading in this new voice. The changes will not become natural overnight. But as you continue with all your vocal exercises and practice speaking from a different pitch placement, you are on the road to your WOW! when it comes to your sound.

HOW PEOPLE RECEIVE YOUR SOUND

Another area that's especially important when we talk about vocal behavior is subtext. Think of subtext this way—messages you send beyond the words you speak. This component of vocal behavior focuses on how people receive your sound. And by this, I mean the sound of your voice plus your entire vocal presence. At this point, it's important that you've already started to work on vocal health and vocal exercises. The focus on the health and fine-tuning of your larynx will help you have a more powerful presence and delivery of your vocal behavior.

Subtext

One way I showcase subtext to my clients is to act out the "annoying, ditzy Roshini character." It's always very off-putting to them because she sounds airy and nasally. She's hard to listen to and, because of the sound of her voice, does not sound credible. Remember, I hold myself out as a communication consultant. In that role, you should and would expect someone with a strong voice, professional look, and expertise on presentation. When you hear "ditzy Roshini," that doesn't spell credibility for how I put myself in the marketplace. So at that point, if my vocal behavior is less than credible, it really doesn't matter how I look or what I know. The subtext my receiver is hearing says *not credible.*

Put this example into your world. Are you a banker? Are you a general contractor? Are you a teacher? Imagine a banker who sounds flighty. Would you trust her with your life savings? No matter how powerful her suit looked, you would think twice. Imagine a contractor who sounds like he doesn't know the difference between concrete and dry wall. Would you trust him with your house? Imagine the teacher who is trying to teach multiplication but does so using a bunch of slang with no control over grammar. You might be so distracted by her delivery, which in this case is her vocal behavior, that you can't focus on the content she's actually trying to teach. Her vocal behavior did not fit what you expect from a teacher. Your vocal behavior helps you play the role you call yourself in the business world. If your listener receives your vocal behavior with anything less than credibility, you are not on the road to gaining a client, selling your goods, or sounding like an expert.

Your vocal behavior is more than just your voice. To my mind, it's the most important part of a powerful performance. It doesn't matter what you know, if you don't know how to present it. A powerful performance requires you to embody the role you claim. Strong vocal behavior can only help your overall performance. And weak vocal behavior is a danger to your intent.

You don't want to hurt all the work you've put into following the I-A-P™ Formula only to lose it to a weak vocal behavior. When you have strong and authoritative vocal behavior, you help your body position itself for great posture and effective body language. It all works together.

TOOLBOX TALK

1. **Your vocal behavior consists of three parts:**
   - **a. How you sound**
   - **b. How you deliver your sound**
   - **c. How people receive your sound**
2. **Be mindful of vocal health: hydration, diet, rest for your larynx**
3. **Do weekly vocal exercises; the yawn is the most basic and transportable**
4. **Remember your vocal behavior sends out subtextual messages that go beyond the words you speak**

CHAPTER 13

BODY LANGUAGE AND BEYOND

By now you know one of my mantras: It doesn't really matter what you *know* if you don't know how to *present* it. You can have a great image and terrific vocal behavior. But if you are awkward with your body, you ultimately won't deliver well. And this goes whether the audience sees you in-person, on a screen, or hears you in some audio format. Even if you're giving a teleseminar or leaving an important voice mail message, whatever your body is doing will affect and influence your entire ability to perform. So let's consider your body language.

YOUR POSE

What kind of model are you? Do you strut the runway—your presentation stage? Or, do you stand stiff and lifeless similar to mannequin models holding clothes on their frames in the department store? Both of these are probably extremes when it comes to your presentation moments. But they can help you understand and visualize what would be positive and successful use of your body and body movement, and on the other hand, what could be detrimental.

The Mannequin

You know people who are like the mannequin model. You may see them in your normal course of life or when you go out to watch a presentation of any kind. You wonder if these mannequins ever blink. They are rigid with their bodies. Their lack of movement affects their entire presentation moment. When your body is stiff, you greatly reduce your tools for bringing your content to life.

The Negatives: When your body has little life, you make it difficult to sound enthusiastic or interesting with your subject matter. It's difficult to actually get your voice or expression to showcase anything but stiff. Your body movement affects your ability to deliver words and look good visually. Distraction can come in the form of being too rigid, so people are focused on your stiffness rather than actually listening to you. Distraction of any kind is something to avoid. You've heard the saying "you are what you eat." Well, in this case, you present as comfortably as your body feels. And when your body feels stiff, the finished product doesn't get any better than what you feed it.

The Positives: You'll never get me to say there's anything positive about being rigid and stiff. But I will say a dose of *stillness* doesn't hurt in your mix of presentation tools. Sometimes just stopping and using no movement can be a way of pacing yourself and your presentation. Getting everyone to focus attention on you as a steady rock can be highly effective. Just make sure you don't confuse this with lifelessness or a constant state of mannequin model.

The Runway Model

Taken to an extreme, the runway model presenter can be a little over the top. She struts around on stage or on the big screen as if running a race or singing at a rock concert. In other words, the fact that she's moving excessively is actually distracting. There are negative and positive aspects of the runway model movement style. It's important for you to know the difference.

The Negatives: You want to avoid distraction of any kind when you present. And actually, excessive movement can affect your ability to present well and hurts your audience's ability to focus and listen to you. That's when the runway model style becomes a distraction. You may notice some people who seem to move their head with every word. That's not good delivery. Each word in every sentence doesn't need or deserve emphasis. By moving your head with each word, one subtextual message you send is you haven't bothered to identify which part of your content—which words—really deserve or need emphasis.

The Positives: The effective part of the runway model has to do with performance imagery. If you believe you're on a stage looking sharp and standing tall, you're more likely to exude confidence and perform powerfully. Comedian Chris Rock once shared a story of being inspired by his mentor Richard Pryor. Rock shared how Pryor was one of the first in the comedy business to move around on stage. The movement kept his audience sharp. Rock explained how he incorporated this into his own style and described how the movement made him a moving target. And that also meant his audience would stay engaged by having to watch Rock move around instead of falling asleep if he were to stand in one place. Chris Rock uses movement effectively. The problems arise when people use too much movement and get too distracting. But movement used in line with your personality type and in a good dose can be a powerful presentation strategy.

ROCK STAR MOMENTS

Someone once asked me what my long shot dream career would be. As much as I love what I do and wouldn't change it, I admitted that I could handle the life of a rock star. I'm talking an actual rock star who gets on a stage and sings, jams with her band, and dances around in front of thousands in a packed coliseum. Okay, I'll stop with the fantasy. But my guess is many people would love the life. The fact is, singing in front of thousands will never be my life given my singing voice. But I use rock star imagery as a guide for my own keynote speaking as well as a way to help my clients focus on getting to their WOW!

Moving away from the musical arena, the rock star I speak of is a unique individual in his or her own field. I want you to start thinking of yourself as the rock star. Others want advice from you. Your competitors dream of surpassing your success. Your friends revel in your fabulous-ness. The fact is, most rock stars aren't born that way. This rock star status I want you to visualize and become takes some planning, practice, and of course, intent. In the world of your presentation moments, here's some guidance to integrate rock star thinking into your habits and practice.

Get Off Notes—Focus on Words

It sounds so simple: Get off your written notes. Focus on your spoken words. But it's amazing how many people decide they should script verbatim everything they hope to say during their presentation. Once I was at an annual event for a large national non-profit, and the board chair was a main speaker during the program. Early in her talk, she missed some words in her script, pointed out her mistake to the audience, and then couldn't find her place again. She managed to make jokes about the script before moving on but not until a few separate moments of dead silence and a few moments of visually paging through her script and, from what I could tell, having to just dump out of a part of it. How you present your content directly reflects your credibility. The more polished and poised you present your message, the better your chance for success. This board chair lost credibility not so much because she lost her place but rather because her recovery from losing her place was flustered, awkward for the audience, and showcased an unpoised leader. She was uncomfortable. The audience was uncomfortable. This scenario need not happen to you.

Transcripts do not have to be a bad thing. But they rarely, if ever, should accompany you to the podium or location of your presentation moment. One way a transcript can be helpful is during your pre-show preparation. I sometimes will write out my presentation moment verbatim as a tool for review. I go over it many times. Then I boil the transcript down into an outline. I ultimately bring the outline down to a few bullet points on a note card or one-sheet. The mere fact that I practiced with a transcript helps when I look at those bullet points and construct sentences partly from in-the-moment ad lib and partly from rehearsing with a verbatim transcript.

Showcase Your Production

Rock stars also put some time into preparing for their specific audience and know how to vary their interactive moments and vocal pacing for each presentation moment. Thinking about audience focus and pacing will put you ahead of other presenters. Using this preparation effectively will win you legions of fans.

AUDIENCE FOCUS

During the Audience Analysis work you did earlier with the I-A-P™ Formula, you figured out what kind of audience will experience you. You asked yourself, "Who are these people?" and you came up with some answers. Now, during the Powerful Performance part of the formula, you get to put all that knowledge and data into practice and deliver.

When you focus on a particular audience, you may see that you're customizing your content to really get through to this individual audience. Your audience may be one person or one hundred. As I often say, *you* don't change, but *your audience* does. Your expertise doesn't waiver, but you may need to change up how you deliver your content to any particular audience in order to make sure they understand you. Anything you can do to showcase to your audience that you aren't a one-size-fits-all kind of presenter will help you deliver powerfully. Maybe that means having oranges available to a group of citrus growers or prizes wrapped in cartoon paper for a group of clowns. You get the picture. You're focusing on this particular audience and delivering your content in the best way to get them to hear and understand you. Think about your favorite music (rock) star. The good ones make each audience feel like the audience they're in front of is the only audience they entertain.

PACING

Thinking about pacing and using various pacing devices will also help you look and sound like a rock star. The easiest way for me to describe pacing is to ask you to think about some of the monotone presenters you've heard. How boring and distracting can it be when these people use a monotone sound and have no variation or creativity in their delivery? The problem is they lack pacing, and it hurts them big time. Some pacing devices for your toolbox include varying vocal loudness or softness, speeding up or slowing down your rate of speech, using an anecdote, sharing a story, quoting a great line. Have fun with trying these and coming up with your own.

CHOREOGRAPHY

As you decide how to showcase your content, I suggest a sort of mini choreography for your presentation moment. One example: You may figure out where in the outline of your presentation you want to include an interactive exercise with one member of your audience or with a small group. If you're in a teleseminar scenario, you may ask your participants to stand up and do something in their respective spaces. No one can see each other, so this won't be embarrassing. That's not to say you can't do this if everyone's in the same room. The point is you are making some predetermined time in your presentation moment to move away from you speaking to your group and letting yourself interact with your group or audience members interact with one another.

Presenters need to be comfortable with their subject matter in order to choreograph audience interaction. When you choreograph with purpose, you're perceived as comfortable enough to go off script or involve the audience. This enables the audience to decide you are a rock star—even if they don't use that exact term.

I always suggest you make interactives fit the group and the subject matter you're covering. By varying things up and planning for different pacing devices, you will have a smoother outcome. That smooth outcome will convey rock star qualities to your audience.

VOCAL VARIATION

A couple of my favorite pacing devices are varying the loudness or softness of your voice and changing the rate at which words flow out of your mouth. The volume of your words and the speed at which you say them can be very effective in keeping your audience awake and engaged. Think about how teachers sometimes speak in a lower volume voice. This subconsciously gets their students to think they better listen up, or they'll miss something important. You can use the soft voice technique to draw your own points. I just suggest you don't overuse it.

Similarly, you can get louder during an important line, or speed your delivery, or slow it down. I recommend you do *not* try all of these pacing devices in one presentation moment if you're not used to them. Take one or two at a time and incorporate them into your next presentation moment. As you start using them and become comfortable with them, you will naturally use them. At some point, they'll become automatic. You'll develop your own style that will include these pacing devices.

PRACTICE MAKES PERFECT

Your piano teacher said it. Your mom reminded you. Your baseball coach repeated the mantra. Practice makes perfect is a phrase you've heard throughout life. And with all things presentation, there's no real substitute for this expression. You can read this book and take in all the Toolbox Talk, but if you do not put your new presentation tools into use, you will not improve as a presenter. It's that simple. I always recommend baby steps. I also suggest you monitor yourself. How do you keep track of your progress? You use playback and record data from each presentation moment.

Playback

One way to collect data about your presentation moments is videotape. Videotape can be a great self-teacher. By watching yourself and reviewing your presentation moments with Toolbox Talk in mind, you should be able to measure your progress. You can see whether you're doing something weird with your eyes or how certain colors look on you. Audio recordings can work in a similar way when you want to focus on vocal behavior review.

Your videotape or audio tape or digital recording does not have to be fancy. The key to practice making perfect is playback and review. There's nothing like seeing or hearing yourself after you delivered your presentation moment.

During my life in TV news, I watched my playback often. After you get over the initial discomfort, it becomes natural to watch yourself objectively and for constructive feedback. I promise you will get over that strange feeling of being on some kind of voyeuristic endeavor. Trust me on this. And really, the difference between fair or good performers and powerful performers is the ability to stick with and improve WOW! moments and work around challenges. There's no better way to figure this out than to watch and/or listen to your own performances. To the extent you need an expert to help you review, I advise you get some professional help. I share some options for connecting with this help in the back of the book. (See Helpful Connections.)

Presentation Journal

One activity I assign my clients is the presentation journal. It's fun and easy and truly a good way to collect data about yourself. Just as some fitness experts and personal trainers advise you to keep a food journal or as runners keep runners' logs, the presentation journal can be a great tool on the road to your WOW!

With the I-A-P™ Formula, I am teaching you how to analyze yourself and all things connected to your communication skills. To keep that analysis going, we need data. And the presentation journal becomes an inexpensive yet rich tool for self-analysis. My clients share their data with me, so it also is a great tool for me to help them.

There's no right or wrong way to keep your presentation journal, but I have some suggestions. You may keep your journal on your computer, in a notebook by the side of your bed, or in a fancy leather-bound book. No matter which form you choose, one thing is the same—this is your personal record-keeping tool. I tell my clients that the only other person who sees their journals is me, to the extent they are willing to share it. It's a good spot for brainstorming for future presentation moments too. And its multi-dimensional purpose is to help you analyze any presentation moment you've given, work on improving what didn't work, and repeat what did turn out well.

Again, *how* you record your data is your business. But I do suggest you jot things down within the same day of your presentation moment—if not directly afterward, at least by the end of the day you gave it. Think of each presentation moment as a journal entry. Record the date of the presentation moment, its time of day, the weather on that day—if you'd like to figure out how weather affects your ability to present. Be sure to include the *type* of presentation moment you had and to what *type of audience*. For example: keynote to one hundred, one-to-one client prospect meeting, or employee review session.

From there, this is your gig. To my clients, I suggest they include quotes or stories or jokes that worked. I also suggest they write down when things didn't go exactly as planned as well as how they choreographed a particular presentation moment. This way, they can review their entries and figure out if a certain example is worth using again or if they should ditch it. I offer the same advice to you.

You can also use your presentation journal to I-A-P™ your presentation moments before they happen. This is a good tool to start your preparation and keep focused on your intent.

I include some sample entries to get you started:

I. **Keynote to 500 people**

-XYZ's Annual Convention

-10:00 a.m. Tuesday, March 15, 20__

-Cloudy outside but no windows in auditorium

-Audience Notations: mostly sales people and top execs at XYZ

-Used story about my first meeting with XYZ owner on the golf course—story went over well

-Future Notes: next time try to remember more of the names of others I met early on at XYZ to drop into presentation

II. **Sales Presentation to 20**

I = Get Repeat Business from these current clients

A = Heritage Graphics Sales Team

P = Hand out new client gifts during the first part of my presentation to hit home the importance of being interactive with prospects; wear power navy jacket

Scheduled for next week: June 1, 20__

III. **One-to-one session with new customer**

Brilliant Bounce's Corporate Offices

December 1, 20__

9:00 a.m.

Food Notes:

-Ate eggs for breakfast and had upset stomach throughout session

-Note to self: No eggs before presentation moments in the future

-Drank triple espresso at 7:00 a.m.; turned out to be tough on my brain and stomach

-Avoid caffeine prior to any future presentation moments

You see there are lots of options for how you choose to keep, and ultimately use, your presentation journal. You can be as low-tech or high-tech as you want to be with it. The important thing is that you *keep* a presentation journal. It is a great data collection tool. I suggest you look back on it every quarter and at the end of every year and chart your progress as a presenter. How close to your WOW! are you? When you're honest with yourself in your presentation journal, you can honestly answer that question. You can also use your presentation journal to help any presentation expert you may work with to help you get better. When I review presentation journals with my clients and they share things that worked and didn't, I'm in a better position to help them answer the question *why* something was effective or not. Having data there in print instead of relying on their sketchy memories helps me help them. Also, when they journal that something felt good or felt bad, worked or didn't work, they may not actually realize why. When I can track *how* they went about doing something by how thoroughly they keep their presentation journal, I can diagnose the issues or successes and give them a prescription for what comes next on their journey to WOW!

TOOLBOX TALK

1. Find an authentic ready stance; incorporate body movement without going overboard
2. Pacing devices include: stories, anecdotes, quotes, vocal variation
3. Videotape or audiotape your presentation moments
4. Review your recorded presentation moments; keep your analysis in your presentation journal
5. Read and study your presentation journal on a regular basis

CHAPTER 14

DYNAMIC PRESENCE

What makes someone an amazing presenter? As we've seen, many things. But some people do have a leg up on others in the powerful performance department. The French call it *Je ne sais crois.* Many others call it charisma. No matter the label, a dynamic presence can help anyone be a more powerful presenter.

Whether you have natural dynamism or not, I can help you key into dynamic presence to get to your WOW! I will get you on the road, so you can get to your WOW! in a much more authentic way.

IF YA GOT IT, YA GOT IT

Self-perception is where anyone's ability to perform starts. It follows that powerful performance comes from a strong and positive self-perception. In fact, at the very basic level, self-perception is the seed of success or failure. If you have confidence in your abilities, no matter what your knowledge level, you can present well. How you see yourself as a member of your family, your company, society will have direct effects on your presentation moments.

So if you are a confident and dynamic person, don't hide it. If you're unique and highly in touch with your authenticity, let that be your inspiration for powerful performance.

In other words, if ya got it, ya got it. And if ya got it, use it. Use that dynamism to endear your audience to you. Use your dynamism to solidify your content knowledge and credibility. You don't have to apologize for your natural dynamism. If you think you have it but feel a little uneasy about *how* to use it in presentation moments, review the Toolbox Talk from this section. Everything you need to get to your WOW! is here. And to put it in *less-is-more* phraseology: Focus on being yourself. If you have a sense of humor, use it during your interactive moments. If you're known for sharing your love of aviation in an eloquent manner, figure out a way to incorporate those stories and aviation analogies into whatever content you're going to deliver in your next presentation moment. If you're known for something peculiar or strange, try poking fun at it and getting your audience to get you in your own authentic way.

IF YA DON'T, TRY THIS

Perhaps you've decided you are *not* naturally dynamic. That's okay. I applaud you for your honesty. But don't hang your head and think there's no hope. Let me help you tap into a security blanket of sorts—something that could help you start to get on the road not only to your WOW!, but also to your hidden dynamism.

I call it the Authenticity Exercise. There are a couple different ways you could do this, but here's a short version that's both fun and enlightening. Try it when you have some time.

Form: First, pick three people in your life who know you well. These are people with whom you feel most comfortable. They should be people with whom you do not have to edit how you speak or behave, and they are also people you count on to be honest with you. Next, ask each one of them separately to give you three words that describe you. Make note of those words and put them into a list—preferably in your presentation journal. Compare these words. Notice if there are word similarities among the three authenticity-exercise friends. If so, great. If not, don't worry.

Self-Analysis: Now from your complete list of words, select three words that best describe you. These three words = your Authentic Self.

Benefits: Should you ever find yourself uneasy about an upcoming presentation moment or a little nervous about *how* a presentation is going *while* you're delivering it, you can call on your Authentic Self. Think of your Authentic Self as your security blanket. We usually need a security blanket when things are off balance and not usually when things are rolling smoothly. Some people might call this a personal brand. No matter the label. When in doubt, let your Authentic Self guide you.

For example, I'll share my Authentic Self words. Most people who know me would say I'm passionate, intelligent, and like to have fun. Okay, so the last one's a phrase. The point is if I'm ever having trouble being inspired or feel myself getting uncomfortable mid-presentation, I focus my brain on my security blanket words. I do *not* try to be someone I'm not when uneasy feelings arise before or during a presentation moment. By fixating on my Authentic Self, I get myself back into the right frame of mind to deliver powerfully.

LEAVE 'EM WANTING MORE

By now you know I love the expression *less is more*. I mean we probably all want more money, more time, more peace. And more of those things would be truly great and might be some exceptions to my phrase. But in general, we could all use some editing in our lives.

One area where most of us could stand to conserve is our use of language. When I worked in TV news, I had to make less really equal more because one-minute and thirty-second stories (or shorter) were the rule of the day.

Now with my clients, I'm constantly reviewing *less-is-more* strategies, whether that be giving media training and teaching about effective sound bites, or as communication consultant, instructing about re-phrasing $20 words to their more colorful, concise, and conversational cousins.

Whenever I give a presentation myself, I aim to leave my audience wishing I'd go on awhile longer. I aim and hope to deliver so effectively they don't even realize thirty minutes, sixty minutes, or even more have passed.

To my journalism students, I teach the Elimination List: a, that, the, of. Is every use of these words necessary in your writing? Try reading your document, script, or proposal out loud and see how many words from the Elimination List you can cut. Of course, some the's are a must. But where they're not, why not make fewer the greater way to phrase?

The main thing is to make sure the performance of your intent after careful audience analysis is the right amount of content, with that content delivered in as crisp a way as you can deliver it. Visualize wrapping up feeling you've powerfully performed great information for your audience, but you've also left them room to want more. They may get their additional thirst through asking you questions post-performance, dropping you a line another day, or asking you to return for an entirely new time frame.

When you can release any urge to pack your presentation so full that there's no breathing room, you put yourself on the path to success and fulfilling your intent. But when you pack it, you risk losing your audience entirely. *Less is more.*

CHARISMA

Some people are blessed with charisma. Others develop it over a life well-lived. And for some, charismatic behavior will elude them their entire lives. No matter which group you fall into, you can use charisma and charismatic people to inspire you with your presentation moments. Your dictionary can give you a formal definition for charisma. But charisma is truly one of the toughest words to adequately define.

In public life, you can probably think of people with charisma. Sometimes it's quiet. Sometimes the charisma is more outgoing. Actors such as Audrey Hepburn, Humphrey Bogart, and Gregory Peck will go down in Hollywood history as charismatic figures and for different reasons. Each one of them conjures up a certain elegance and style that came through in their performances. Everyone agrees they had *charisma*.

You probably know people in your business and social circles who possess natural charisma too. Some of them use it as a presentation tool, and others don't even realize they're drawing on it to win friends wherever they go.

I was blessed to have two parents with a natural charisma. Perhaps watching them over time became instilled in my brain and has allowed me to draw on that inspiration. Their charisma inspires me in my work and play—whether in my keynote speaking, consulting my clients, or planning a party.

To you, my dear reader, I want to help you think about charisma as an extra communication tool. Consequently, no matter where you fall on the charisma spectrum, you can use the concept to grow your own dynamic presence. Let yourself be inspired by others. Watch and seek out people you do believe are charismatic. Study their mannerisms and communication styles. Apply the skills you are working on and the tools you are learning here because you can control those. Over time you will see that your charisma quotient will indeed go up. And really all you can ever do is practice.

Powerful presentation and WOW! moments don't just happen. They are things you create by staying authentic and being in tune with you own self-perception. WOW! moments come from practice and a dedicated approach to inspiring and informing others. Be intentional and you will get better. Create some effective presentation moments, and you will inspire yourself to create more. As they say in golf, "You're only as good as your last shot." In TV news, they often say, "You're only as good as your last story." Take these adages as a source of inspiration and realize your last powerful performance can help you in the future. Because each time you have a WOW! moment, you put yourself in position to have more of them.

TOOLBOX TALK

1. **Make sure your self-perception is positive and strong**
2. **If you have natural dynamism, use it**
3. **No matter what, remain authentic**
4. **Leave 'em wanting more by using *less is more* as a theme for your preparation**

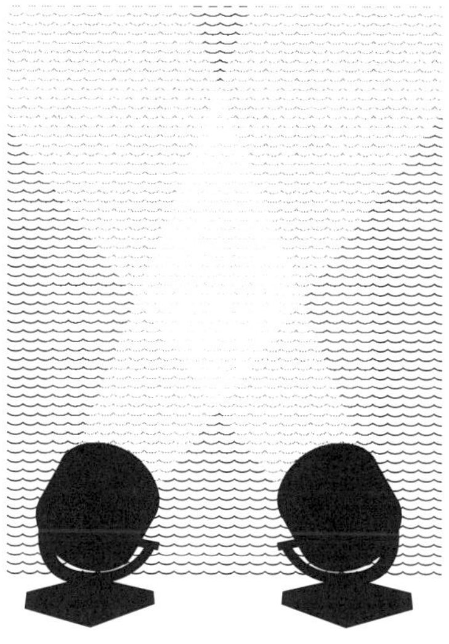

SECTION IV

YOU HAVE IT, FLAUNT IT

Using the I-A-P™ Toolbox

CHAPTER 15

BUSINESS DEVELOPMENT

I joked about commitment phobia at the beginning of this book. I'm going to remind you about it here. In the dating world, an unwillingness to commit can range from comical to downright tragic. Let's just say the same is true with your presentation moments if you don't commit to applying, using, and practicing your new presentation toolbox—the I-A-P™ Formula. You now know what each part of the I-A-P™ Formula means and entails because of your careful reading of the three previous sections. You've got the toolbox. You even have highlights from each section at the end of each chapter in the form of Toolbox Talk. Now use the formula and let Toolbox Talk be your quick reference guides.

In the world of business development, I-A-P™ can be your friend. I'm going to walk you through some common business settings with the help of the I-A-P™ Formula. Focusing on it instead of thinking negatively or fearing the upcoming presentation moment can get you to your WOW!

NETWORKING

The term is one that should be familiar to you even if you don't regularly attend networking events. Many deals launch or get done because of people's smart networking skills. One spring I got a lead on a new local client from someone who used to intern for me at a past TV station. The young man recommended me to a business associate he knew from his public relations post in another state. How cool is that? But the power of the network is only as powerful as your ability to deliver. The desire for you or your colleagues to network on one another's behalf is only as strong as the powerful presentation moments you put out there.

Deliver your content, deliver your personality, deliver your word. When I recommend someone, I only do it because I'm quite sure the person I'm recommending will do a good job and also represent me well. That person will deliver his or her best and make me look good. Everyone's happy when the connection shakes down as anticipated. And to deliver strongly, try using your I-A-P™ Toolbox. Just rely on each of the letters of the formula as you approach future networking opportunities.

Let's start with ***Intent***. Before you arrive at your networking event, you should have a game plan. Do some work on your intent, so you have a road map for what you're trying to accomplish. If you're attending a Rotary Club lunch and have thirty seconds to introduce yourself, focus your intent. You should make every second count and not even waste a sentence. Realize there are seventy other people in the room who'll also get thirty seconds. What can you say that will really be memorable? If you're focused and think through your intent ahead of time, you can make every word count; you can perform powerfully. And realize it took about thirty seconds to read this paragraph. So that's all the time you have in many cases. Not a lot of words. *Less is more.*

Audience Analysis: Who's your audience? Who will you be meeting and speaking with? If they're a bunch of bankers who are watching the clock before you get there, that's a different type of audience and attention span than Procrastinators Anonymous or the National Clown Association's annual convention. Let your intent guide you to tailor your content to this audience.

Powerful Performance: You make it all come together when you perform your intent with any particular audience powerfully. That means you're not high on coffee or looking drowsy from a night of no sleep. That means your voice is projecting strongly without being domineering. If you know you have a soft voice and the meeting is in a large space, perhaps you need to find a microphone to use to do your introduction. Of course, get that detail in order before your presentation moment begins. Powerful performance also means you look polished and clean. You will not represent yourself or your company well in a group of other business people by looking rumpled. And as far as *what* you do say, don't try to pack in a novel's worth of words where a few bullet points will do.

There are likely as many different kinds of networking events as there are people who attend them. The point is to figure out what you're doing before you get there. Let the I-A-P™ Formula be your friend and use it.

GIVING INTRODUCTIONS

Now that I've identified one type of arena—networking—where you can use the I-A-P™ Formula to introduce yourself, let's actually focus on those introductions. What will you say and how will you say it? Just I-A-P™ it.

Who Are You?—Your Own Introduction

I often tell my clients, you can't even get to the sale or the product or the service you're offering, if you don't hook them on *you* and your credibility. And the first place to start your successful business connection is to introduce yourself powerfully. Imagine you're at the annual luncheon of a group you support, and you know it's a prime place for networking. I'm guessing you've been in this or a similar situation already.

You be the judge. How does it come across when someone has a weak handshake, a weak appearance (messy, dirty, unprofessional), a weak introduction? You probably question his or her ability to be the professional he or she claims to be. I'll take an example that seems obvious for purposes of illustration. In your encounters, this person could be male or female. For now, let's say you meet a businesswoman who claims to be a personal clothes shopper for high-level executives, yet she looks as if she doesn't regularly wash her hair and seems to have an overall unkempt appearance. Would you want to hire her as your personal shopper? I would hope not! Her appearance betrayed her. Additionally, she introduced herself in a stream-of-consciousness sort of way, so you also doubt her ability to communicate with you.

Her weak introduction, subtextually, also puts into question whether she has any expertise in the area she's trying to get your business. You probably won't even talk about that now because you're put off by the introduction.

I don't want *you* to be the business person with such a weak first impression. Let's work on how you would I-A-P™ any introduction of yourself. Assume someone is asking: Who Are You? Then use the I-A-P™ Formula to solidify that you know who you are and you know what you know.

Intent: The journalist in me suggests you think of some basic W's asked in most media interviews.

Who? What? Why?

Who am I?—Make an honest and authentic assessment. Then along with your name, say something, or write something, interesting.

What is my purpose?—Focus on the particular introduction every time. Do not go generic. What am I trying to get across about myself and/or what I do with this introduction?

Why do I want this group/person to hear me?—By connecting the *Why* as you plan your intent for this introduction, you give yourself the ability to keep things simple and not over-complicate a basic, yet powerful, introduction. I like to say one size does *not* fit all when it comes to introductions. I'm *not* a fan of what is labeled the elevator speech, elevator pitch, or individual commercial. Those terms ignore the fact that with each introduction to each specific audience, you have the opportunity to powerfully introduce yourself in a way that speaks to them specifically. You have the unique opportunity to WOW!

Audience Analysis: The W's here are Who? When? Where?

Who are these people?—Identify the particular audience this particular introduction will be presented to. By knowing to whom you're speaking, you set yourself up for a powerful performance.

When am I speaking?—Know when you will give this introduction. Is it a morning, an afternoon, an evening? Different times of the day present some individual choices you'll make as to how you will interact within your own abilities. Some people are better in the morning. Some are more relaxed and powerful in the evening. Sometimes you can't control the *When* but knowing more about it will help you give a more focused introduction that's appropriate for that time of day or crowd.

Where will I be?—Location, location, location. Are you going to be in an auditorium, a small function room, or an individual office? Are you speaking at an architects convention or to the National Association of University Presidents? Are you in Texas or New York? Your location may also inform what type of introduction is best.

Powerful Performance: And the journalistic H question—How?

This is when you put all your planning together by bringing a strong look, sound, and your authentic self together.

Ask yourself, *How can I use my powerful presentation skills to showcase myself?*

Image—People make their first impression of you within seconds. You do not want to risk losing them before you open your mouth. Make sure you look good. Make sure your hair style is in place, whether you are a man or woman. For that matter, make sure there's some style to your hair. Have the good sense to double-check there's no food in your teeth before you speak to the person or group you will meet.

I explain the idea of the power outfit to my clients this way. You know you have one or two at least. So wear one of them. There is no absolute definition of a power outfit. But I'll give you a broad idea. Your power outfit makes you look good and credible in the position you are trying to portray. It fits nicely and flatters your size and shape. No matter where it falls in the conservative attire to trendy spectrum, the colors are good for you. When you know you need to make your self-introduction count, why not wear something that gives you extra confidence? Your power outfit will help you look good and communicate powerfully.

Vocal Behavior—By now you realize your vocal behavior is more than just the sound of your voice. Your vocal tone, personality, volume, and the subtextual messages your vocal behavior sends all contribute to your introduction. There are many times I have to give a short twenty-second introduction at an event. I decide ahead of time that *less is more*. I'm not going to cram everything about myself and my company into that short period of time. I won't even try to paraphrase. Because I spent time to I-A-P™ the introduction before I got there, I have a plan in mind. I also take some time to do some quick vocal exercises on my way to the event. (See chapter twelve for a recap of vocal exercises.)

Authentic—All powerful performance goes back to, and really starts with, self-perception. The stronger and more positive your self-perception, the better your performance. You have the ability to stay strong when you stick with your authentic self. Even in a short introduction, your listeners can decide quickly whether or not you're real.

As I said earlier in the book, I like to say I'm Roshini every day of the week. I'm Roshini for my mother, for my clients, for my friends. The moment you think you have to change who you are is the moment your powerful performance is in danger or not even a possibility. Keep it authentic and true to *you*, and you'll do well.

ART OF THE INTRODUCTION—INTRODUCING OTHERS

When you introduce others, you have two goals to guide your intent. Think of these goals as your duties: 1) Honor the person/subject you're introducing; 2) Showcase yourself as a business person.

What I've noticed in my years of noticing is most business people forget about number two. And often, they pull off a lackluster job with number one. As I continue to teach the I-A-P™ Formula, I realize it's because people do not use or apply I-A-P™ effective preparation techniques to the introductions of others. That's why you should do it.

When you think about introducing others, you probably think about introducing another *person*. But also realize there are things you may be introducing that aren't focused on a person but serve as indirect ways to honor another person.

Three main types of introductions are for a person, a meal, or a celebration.

or you may be doing a straight introduction of a business associate or friend. The regular I-A-P™ Formula applies. I'm also going to add a twist as I give you some guidance on the introduction of others. From my TV news and legal background, we'll call it my version of do's and don'ts—Air This/Strike That.

Air This: Try something new or fresh. Think of something (an award, a sport, a memory, an affiliation) that honors the person you're introducing. Share something from the heart that connects you to the person you're introducing. I suggest you make it something the audience cannot read in the program or something that might not be common knowledge. This also puts you in position to showcase yourself and your knowledge because you're sharing little known or unknown information about your subject. Be sure to pronounce the person's name correctly.

Strike That: Avoid using sheets of paper or reading a bio from someone's Web site. Do not solely use information that's in the written program when you make an individual introduction of someone else. The audience can just read the program for that. Your duty is to honor the person, so give your audience something different. This is also your opportunity to showcase yourself by giving the audience something new and fresh about your subject.

Do the glasses check: If you need glasses to read fine print, and you actually put them on for this introduction of someone else, strike that behavior. Powerful introductions aren't read. They're given with good eye contact and strong delivery. If you need something in hand, make it a note card with a few bullet points. And by all means, do not think you're going to wing it. This can lead to disasters: losing key points you had hoped to make, forgetting about something the person you're introducing wanted you to include, looking sloppy and unprofessional.

Meal

You may have the fun or serious role of welcoming a group at a meal. This introduction could take multiple forms. Perhaps you introduce a person who then runs the meal. Perhaps you introduce a team. Perhaps your introduction is actually a toast or a prayer before a meal.

Your intent should be to honor the group, or a person, or the day itself as you introduce this meal.

Air This: If you possess comedic skills, use them. That can be fun or fresh. Words of honor can be your own. Or you can draw on the multiple quote and prayer books on the market. Will an Irish limerick do the trick? If it won't offend anyone and fits with your audience, go for it. Remember there's a reason you were asked to give this particular introduction. For example, maybe that fact itself could inspire your content. Ask yourself if you have a personal connection to this group or the event and work that into your introduction.

Strike That: This type of introduction might make for a more difficult one to do off the top of your head. If you can do it without sheets of paper, try to. If you need a crutch to keep you from forgetting key points, a small note card with bullet points is preferable. Remember, you don't want to belabor what you're saying when you introduce a meal. People want to eat! *Less is more.*

Celebration

An introduction at a celebratory event should prove fun and rewarding. Two forms this could take are the event welcome and the announcement during an event. Remember, you are part of the program. So what you do and say affect how the audience remembers this event. Yes, it can be daunting. But when you I-A-P™ it, you'll be in a better position to leave a positive legacy.

Air This: In some cases, you are introducing or welcoming people to an event that has happened annually. You'll want to make your introduction new and fresh. Again, think about honoring someone or some people involved with the celebration. Perhaps there will be an award coming up for Volunteer of the Year. Share a fun moment you had with that person or something about them you've researched or know that isn't common knowledge.

If this is a first-event-of-its-kind celebration, then you have the gift of being able to really make this introduction authentically yours. The same rules apply though. What can you say or do with the introduction to make it unique? Also, in I-A-P™ fashion, decide what your intent is before you outline your introduction. For instance, I was asked to emcee the twenty-first anniversary party for a friend, client, and advisor who was celebrating her years of owning her own law firm. I helped her come up with the idea of calling it the "21 Years Legal Party." She was able to use that as a theme for the event, from the invitations to the gift bags guests received as they walked out. I also used that theme as a guide for my emcee duties.

As her emcee, my first agenda item was to properly welcome people to the event while guests were settling in. My friend is the biggest part of the brand because it's her law firm, so I decided my intent was to honor her as I welcomed guests to the celebration. But I also knew she wanted to honor key people who helped her reach the milestone, so I worked that into connectors between the various parts of the program. I could not have done the things I did as emcee if I hadn't gone over the I-A-P™ Formula with her ahead of time to plot out goals for the entire celebration.

If you're asked to give a special announcement within a celebration, you still want to I-A-P™ it. Perhaps this introduction is for an award. Perhaps it's to highlight a group in the community the organizers want to thank for a donation. Perhaps it's to introduce a video at the event that showcases the past year's activity. Your role here is to introduce or guide the audience through a specific spot within the celebration agenda. Realize you have control over making this a special performance. Keep to your time limit but make your introduction unique and memorable. Share a quote. Share a story. Share a secret passion you have for this organization. Whatever your angle, keep it fresh and from the heart.

Strike That: Sheets of paper and too much written information can torpedo a strong performance when you are asked to make either type of celebration introduction. As the person giving the introduction, it should appear obvious to your audience that you know the event, group, or honoree you're introducing at the celebration. Even if you don't have a lot of background, you can't go to the microphone and blow an introduction like this because of lack of research or unfamiliarity. So be sure to do your homework. If you don't have time to do it, ask planners or your co-workers to help you with background. With all introductions, your first job is to honor the subject of your introduction, and second, showcase yourself as a business person. I-A-P™ is your friend here. Use it.

I-A-P™ AT THE WORKPLACE

You now have some guidance on using the I-A-P™ Formula with your networking efforts and with making introductions of yourself and others. Those areas will help you build your profile as a business person and bring in more opportunities. But what about when you're involved with day-to-day activities at the workplace? You have several opportunities to use the I-A-P™ Formula to help make you a more polished and memorable business person. In turn, you can grow your reputation with your colleagues as well as with your clients and potential customers. Don't lose numerous daily opportunities to showcase yourself and your business acumen. Just I-A-P™ it.

Voice Mail

I often ask my potential clients, how much business are you gaining or losing because of your voice mail? If you're like most business people, your voice mail greets more people in a day than you do personally. Less is definitely more here. But without a clear focus on what you're doing with that voice mail, less or more could be disastrous.

Say it with me, just I-A-P™ it. Every business person should focus on outgoing greetings as a form of business communication. When I include voice mail consultations as part of my business seminars, people usually are inspired to make this plan for when they return to the office: 1) Listen to voice mail message; 2) Re-record voice mail message.

Before you re-record, I-A-P™ the end result. And when you listen to the outgoing greeting, analyze before you press save.

Here are some quick tips for analyzing your voice on your business greeting

1. *Ask yourself: Is this someone with whom I'd do business?*
2. *Identify the vocal behavior you hear in your outgoing greeting.*

3. *Decide if that vocal behavior will help you gain a client, maintain a client, lose a client, or insult a prospective client.*

Does the sound of your voice convey the real you?

Once you've answered these questions, you can work on the final version you want for your voice mail greeting. Now, let's I-A-P™ it together.

Intent: You want the answers to question #3 to land on the positive side. So decide what you intend with this voice mail. What do you want your voice mail greeting to really say to anyone hearing it? Are you including some sort of call to action? Do you have separate internal and external versions? Make an intent for each. They may or may not be the same.

Audience Analysis: Determining and remembering who listens to your voice mail greeting will help you focus your content and can help guide your intent. Again, do you have one voice mail greeting or different versions? In most cases, your outgoing external greeting has a multitude of possible listeners. Make sure you keep all or most contingents in mind before you plan to record.

Powerful Performance: As you start and continue to do your vocal exercises, you will also bring a stronger voice to your arsenal. So it's okay if you have several re-records as you continue to develop your vocal performance skills. The important thing is to make the vocal behavior your listener hears as strong as you've got at any moment in time. If it won't make you too stiff and sound like you're reading, I suggest plotting out a short script for your voice mail greeting. Either map out bullet points or write out verbatim text that will help you maximize this short but powerful communication tool.

Meetings

You're going to put time into running a meeting or making a presentation at a meeting, so why not make it powerful. Just I-A-P™ it.

Intent: Whether it's a weekly team meeting, an annual review, or a company training, every business meeting should have a focus. Your colleagues won't know what to expect if you don't. In other words, if you're the one running the meeting and do not know your intent for the meeting, why should your co-workers?

If you're giving a presentation as part of a bigger meeting agenda, your co-workers will not know what you want from them or for them if *you* don't know. A defined intent for any meeting is a must.

Audience Analysis: Not every meeting is the same nor every audience similarly situated. A morning audience of your team members is different from an afternoon audience of everyone in the company. There are personalities of your colleagues to keep in mind, their moods, whether they've eaten before your presentation, whether they're eating during your presentation, and whether refreshments are served after you present. Take the time to understand your specific audience, and you will prepare content that's best suited for it. Remember the audience research you learned how to do in chapter six. Who are these people? When you know who's in front of you, you will do a better job of personalizing the information for them. Think about whether you have special stories about anyone in the audience or some other connection that ties in with your content. For example, a story about a co-worker's success or a quote your boss is known for saying are just two of many ways you can personalize to your specific audience. This audience analysis, in turn, gets you thinking about how to perform well.

Powerful Performance: Once you're clear with your intent and have done your audience analysis, you can deliver your content strategically and powerfully. Will a prop help you describe a new solution you are presenting? Will making everyone get up and get involved with you hit home your point? As outlined in section III, you have many interactive elements available to you. Interactives are one way to go for a powerful performance.

Looking good and sounding good are also important. Show respect for your audience by playing the part and looking like the professional you are. Unless, of course, you're presenting at a costume party or another themed event, make sure your dress code gives the level of respect your business position warrants. If you're a man who hasn't shaved in five days, shave before your presentation moment. Doing regular vocal exercises before game day will really pay off during your presentation moment at any meeting.

Awards

Sometimes you're given the responsibility of presenting an award to a co-worker or employee. Use this opportunity to honor your subject and showcase yourself as a leader. Just I-A-P™ it.

Intent: Really focus your intent on honoring the person or department receiving the award. Don't be generic. Each kind of award or type of business affirmation is different. Make sure your intent focuses on this particular award presentation moment.

Audience Analysis: Again you ask, *who* are these people? Are they people who work directly with the recipient? Is it a mixed group that includes people who don't even know the recipient of the award. Knowing who these people are in front of you will help you shape your content. Plan for any wild cards who might be in the audience. For example, is someone's mother or mentor going to be present to honor the recipient? Figure out how to work that into your content if it's not distracting.

Powerful Performance: Here's your opportunity to really shine. You will honor the award recipient and showcase yourself as a business person. Treat the occasion with dignity when it comes to your appearance and vocal behavior. Will photos be taken of the event? Ask ahead of time, so you can plan the most powerful wardrobe, which is also one that's camera-friendly. Think about technical details (see chapter ten for specific guidance). Make sure you think about choreography and where the photographer will be positioned in terms of you and the award recipient. You don't want the audience's view blocked. But you also want the photographer to get a good perspective if he insists on an action shot.

With all of your business presentation moments, you have the opportunity to really stand out. Use the I-A-P™ Formula to lessen the pressure and produce powerful results. Over time, the formula will not seem like something to do. It will just be a process you follow, and I hope something you just do.

A top sales executive friend once told me when you focus on the process, results will follow. He went on to say when you get caught up in worry about the end result, your process fails. The I-A-P™ Formula is a process. If you follow it instead of stressing about the results it will bring, you should get to many WOW!'s.

Most of what we all do is sales, even if we don't call it that. I devote the next chapter to how the I-A-P™ Formula can serve you well in your unique sales environment.

TOOLBOX TALK

1. **Whether fifteen seconds or four hours, realize any time you want to convince someone of your credibility or sell something to them, you are in a presentation moment**
2. **When introducing yourself, ask:**
    a. **Do I know who I am?**
    b. **Do I know what I know?**
3. **When introducing people or events, remember to:**
    a. **Honor the introduced**
    b. **Showcase yourself**
4. **The I-A-P™ Formula is a process; use it in everyday work settings**

CHAPTER 16

SALES SAVVY

Once you actually break out the I-A-P™ Formula and start using it in all of your presentation moments, it eventually becomes more natural. You'll start to I-A-P™ with ease. This is a good thing when it comes to your ability to sell. Whether that's selling yourself, your company, or your products, the I-A-P™ Formula is your friend and can help you make a mark when it comes to building your reputation as a savvy salesperson.

DIFFERENTIATE

In a world where you're only as good as your last big idea or most recent sales deal, differentiation is a big step toward staying power. Use the I-A-P™ Formula to help you stand out among your peers. If you are one of one hundred car salespeople, what are you going to do to make yourself different? What can you offer that no one else can? Just I-A-P™ it and see how you build your profile. I offer some guidance.

Intent: Think about a recent or future sales call. Whether your sales call is on the phone or in-person, written or beamed out, you have the opportunity to close a deal and hook the potential customer on you and your organization. I advise you not to treat all of these presentation moments the same. Figure out your intent for this particular exchange and let it be your guide. Differentiate among your various sales opportunities. Sound familiar? I hope so. By now you know intent is a key part of my approach and the I-A-P™ Formula's mission. Yes, your intent is co-equal with the other parts of the formula, but it is also the driver. It helps you stay on task and stay focused. The more you clarify and define your intent ahead of time, the more easily you will find success with the daily part of your work life they call selling (yourself, your company, your products).

Audience Analysis: Who are these people? You must understand exactly who your target audience is before you make that sales call. Do your homework. Get a sense of who you already know at that organization. Something as simple as knowing they have a cool new blog on their Web site could go a long way in helping you stand out as someone who checked out your target before you made contact. This may sound simple or obvious. But it's amazing how many people let an organization's Web site go untapped for gaining vital and unique information.

If you're beyond the cold call and about to meet with your target in person, make sure you know the names and titles of the people who will be in front of you. I had a memorable meeting with a high-level female executive at a financial institution. The meeting was in a different city from where my company is based. I didn't leave much to chance. The Internet can be a great tool for finding out vast amounts of information about your target. In this particular case, I learned my contact is really into my favorite band. I didn't get too far into our lunch meeting before mentioning the band. We chatted a little bit about why we like the music. I'm not sure whether it impressed her or not. But you better believe she was on notice that I didn't just show up for the meeting without preparing specifically for her.

Powerful Performance: When it comes to differentiating yourself, the "P" of the I-A-P™ Formula is where you can really get creative. Remember your face, hair, and wardrobe are all part of the image piece of your powerful performance. Your vocal behavior is a key component. And then combining the two with any kind of interactive or take-away for your audience is where you can make some lasting impressions.

Think about the last time you were at a networking event. Who do you remember? My guess is you're saying to yourself, "No one." Or perhaps, "Not many." This is partly because no one's performance stood out. How people introduced themselves was probably business as usual. Even though the "P" is the third part of the I-A-P™ Formula, it is co-equal with the other parts. It is the component of the formula that helps you hit your mark. Your intent drives you, your audience analysis helps you understand in more detail how to shape your content to make it most effective for any particular audience, but the "P" is where you put it all together and deliver—you bring it all home.

Differentiate yourself as a salesperson or business professional by making sure you don't cut corners on performance. Be thorough with your look. Here are some questions I suggest you ask yourself: 1) Am I wearing my power outfit? 2) Does my hair look good? 3) Do I look refreshed or tattered? 4) Will my vocal behavior send out the overt and subtextual messages I intend? 5) What visual aid or small gift will I share to solidify my points in a presentation setting or help them remember me once I leave?

I'll leave it to your own brainstorming in your presentation journal to come up with some other powerful performance questions tailored to your specific presentation style. Just remember that each time you make a distinct decision to fine-tune some aspect of your performance, you are differentiating yourself in the marketplace.

As a licensed attorney, I can say it: Lawyers are a dime a dozen. So what makes the successful ones? Well, they've managed to stand out in their fields by looking good, sounding good, and delivering their message better than their competitors. That scenario is true no matter the profession. You don't have to be an actual professional actor to be judged on your powerful performance. And it all boils down to one of my favorite sayings: It really doesn't matter what you know, if you don't know how to *present* it.

LIVE THE ROLE: TURN BRAND PERFORMANCE INTO MONEY

Taking differentiation to another level, we can talk about your personal brand as a business person. In the marketplace of products, some brands are timeless and quickly recognizable: Coke, McDonald's, Hershey. And consequently, the commitment to brand continues to mean good news at the bank. If you think about it, these companies did their own version of the I-A-P™ Formula to define, build, and instill their brands across the world. Do you think it just happened? Of course not. They had an intent for what they wanted to do with their products and their brands. They analyzed their audiences and figured out needs and wants. And they continue to powerfully perform their differentiation messages with consistent and colorful design graphics, advertisements, and spokespeople.

So with a little inspiration from our food brands, let me help you live your unique role in the marketplace. Depending on your industry, branding can take on several forms. But no matter for whom you work or if you work for yourself, your own personal brand is the place to start with living your role as a professional and building your profile toward more business. Consistent marketing of a unique brand brings bank. Just I-A-P™ it.

Intent: How is it that you want people to view you in the marketplace? A priest or rabbi, for example, likely wants to be known as a religious leader, a counselor, and a person who helps those in need. The brand of priest or rabbi encompasses several aspects we might stereotype in a general sense. But an individual rabbi can move that generic brand a step further by deciding his brand will include a focus on single fathers. Perhaps he becomes known as someone who counsels and advises this particular group of men and has a track record with helping them live fuller lives. You might say that specialty becomes part of his brand. This specialty may have developed accidentally or it may be very intentional.

To the extent you have a brand you want to hold out in the marketplace as unique and showcase yourself as an expert in your field, moving forward with intent is what I advise. Define what it is you want your brand to look like and why. Then move into focusing on the audience you have for this brand. And finally, make sure your delivery of your brand is consistent and powerful.

Audience Analysis: Let's talk about the audience for your brand. Are you a doctor, a banker, a chef? You probably have a sense of who needs your services or wants to buy your products. The more you understand them as current and potential customers, the more successful you will be at getting business leads or making a sale. And in the name of your brand, the more you understand your audience in relation to the intent for your brand, the more loyal customer base you will build.

Your audience needs to see consistency in how you reach out to them. They need to know every time they have an encounter with you or are convinced to buy a service from you, they will get what they're paying for and, more importantly, they need to believe what you're promising.

Powerful Performance: You must deliver your brand with consistency and style. Again, the "P" part of the formula is where you get to live out your intent and your audience analysis. Performing your personal brand can take several forms. Your Web site. Your blog. Your ability to use social media. Your signage. Your collateral material. The list goes on.

The most important aspect for delivery of your brand is consistency that has polish. When I started my company in 2006, I tested about a dozen or more pens before I decided on the one—a simple Pentel black ink pen. As a communication consultant, I didn't want a pen that was leaky or blotchy. It needed to be smooth. It needed to make the user's writing look good. That's the only kind of pen that would match my brand and speak to clients in the way I intend—*present your best.*

A similar story with my business cards and letterhead. I got estimates from five printers and visited my two finalists. The printing company I went with was the farthest distance from my office among the estimates—one state over, in fact—but it was the one that took me in and personally showed me how its team could represent my brand with polish. John Knutson at Resco reminded me that I'm a presentation consultant, so my paper products needed to look great and represent what I offer with consistency and style. The paper products needed to be on quality stock that didn't allow ink to bleed and that didn't look cheap. As a start-up company, my printed materials were my biggest expense. But as it turned out, they were well worth it. I get compliments almost weekly on the sleekness and simplicity of my company logo and the easy-to-write-on card stock of my business cards.

Even though I'm not the most technically inclined, I try to make sure all my written materials, my Web site, and my gift products have a consistent color scheme and look clean and polished. You can give this kind of attention to your powerful performance no matter your budget. It all attests to your brand. A powerful performance in marketing your brand is the best way to showcase the business person you intend to be. And commitment to this consistent marketing, helps you to live your brand powerfully and turn it into dollars.

VOICE MAIL

Outgoing Greetings

I've already described the importance of your outgoing voice mail greeting when it comes to your business development at the workplace. Let's focus further on how to use it to become a more savvy salesperson. Just I-A-P™ it.

Intent: No matter your purpose, I always recommend being intentional with your voice mail. And for the savvy salesperson, focus on showcasing your personality and the very core of who you are as a seller. Define for yourself *what* that person looks like. Remain authentic in your intent. Stay focused and don't attempt too much with this short greeting. Does it make sense to change your greeting daily? Or can one focused greeting deliver a consistent purpose and get across your key points? Only you know the answers to those questions. The important part is you ask the questions while figuring out the intent of your voice mail. A few questions you might use in your analysis are: 1) Should I include the date in this outgoing greeting? 2) Why am I choosing to record this greeting each day? 3) Is it necessary to say my phone number in this greeting when they may have actually dialed it to get to this greeting?

Audience Analysis: Who is going to hear this voice mail greeting? Presumably everyone who calls your direct line, right? If that's not the case, figure out who will hear each outgoing greeting that's attached to your numbers. Is your cell phone greeting the same as the one at your desk? Remember your audience will expect consistency with who you are as a person and a vendor or client of theirs.

Powerful Performance: How you deliver your voice mail greeting is where you get the opportunity to convince your audience of your intent. Scripting out some bullet points you intend to get across is a good idea. You don't necessarily need to read your message from a script. But similar to dancers who choreograph before they perform on stage, it is a good idea to plan out what you will actually say. Practicing this performance is a good idea too. And if you're unsure of any recording, press delete. Re-record. You will thank yourself later.

My personal recommendation is to record your outgoing greeting yourself. Some businesspeople have an assistant or someone else record their greeting. If your intent is to say to your listener that you care about them and want to handle their concerns, not even being present on your voice mail greeting is a turn-off. It sends a subtextual message that is *not* customer-focused.

Messages You Leave Others

Think of voice mail messages you leave for other people as mini presentation moments. You have the opportunity to sell yourself, your company, your product in twenty seconds or less. If you're not trying to make a direct sale with this kind of message, you are at least hoping to hook them enough to return your call. Either way, you want to convince someone of something. Don't be scattered with this great selling tool. Just I-A-P™ it.

Intent: You know you have a fifty-fifty chance of getting the person live when you call. But you also know you have at least a 50 percent chance of missing your target. So that leaves you with enough of a heads-up that you might have to leave a voice mail message. If you've prepared yourself for a possible live phone conversation, you have what you need for a powerful voice mail message. But be sure to decide ahead of time what you'll do if you miss your target. Have a focused intent about what will go into the voice mail message. Be aware that you may have figured out an intent for reaching your target live. That intent may have to change if you reach voice mail because there is not the usual benefit of interaction with a real voice. *Less is more* comes in especially handy when you perform this voice mail greeting.

Audience Analysis: Your listener on the other end of the line is either someone you know well (showtime), know simply (rehearsal), or don't know at all (cold call). Figure that out before you make any call.

Showtime: If you know the person well, you probably know what type of voice mail message the person prefers. You have a sense about whether humor would be appreciated in a voice message or if you should keep things strictly business.

Rehearsal: If you recently met your target or talked with the person once but don't really know his or her personality, you can help yourself by doing a little research about your target prior to placing the call. Perhaps you are already doing this research in preparation for a face-to-face meeting. No matter the case, decide to the best of your ability what kind of relationship you have with the person before you place the call.

Cold Call: You truly have an open slate when it comes to the cold call. You also have your toughest job. Various people have various reactions to people who call them who do not know them. You can't control what they do, but you can do your own audience analysis to make sure what you do decide to say is relevant to your target in some way. Focus on figuring out how to entice this type of audience. Did you recently learn it's a company that's lost millions but wants to save itself from bankruptcy? Well then they probably would react positively to a voice mail message that stresses how much you can help them rebuild their brand. The more audience analysis you put into this type of call, the more successfully you will carry out your intent.

Powerful Performance: Remember *less is more.* This is not only a favorite saying, but also the key to the best voice mail messages you leave others. Think about how many messages you get in a day. Your target probably gets at least as many and perhaps lots more. I offer three words to help guide you: Hook, Showcase, Inspire.

Hook: Enticingly hook your target to take notice of your voice mail message by kicking it off with something original and unique. Perhaps you ask an interesting question to which the target really wants an answer—an answer only you can provide. Perhaps you've focused on powerful vocal behavior through diligent attention to vocal exercises, which makes the subtextual message your vocal behavior conveys in your voice mail message powerful—your target can't wait to call you.

Showcase: Honestly showcase your credibility and what you have to offer your target. For example, use a recent statistic about yourself or your organization that is truly a WOW! for the target.

Inspire: Give them a reason to call you back. Inspire them to want to speak with you. Inspire them to understand you have something that can solve their problems. Inspire them to feel you are the person they need.

FLAUNT IT

I share some of the ways the I-A-P™ Formula can help you become a more polished business person. Similar to the story I shared earlier from a top sales exeucutive, a top saleswoman once told me she doesn't worry about getting the sale as long as she follows the process. I asked her what she meant by that because this was just a few months after I started my business. She said that as long as she follows the steps for making a sale, she lets the process take care of itself. She doesn't allow herself to get stressed about the result of making the sale. She told me she knows if she stays diligent with the process, things should turn out successfully.

Much like my friend's story, think of the I-A-P™ Formula as a process—a process to focused and powerful performance that is fine-tuned to your particular audience. The key is to let go of the nerves and follow the process.

TOOLBOX TALK

1. **Differentiation is key in business; use the I-A-P™ Formula to stand out**
2. **Powerful performance consistency = differentiation and leads to sales/reputation building**
3. **Voice mail greetings and messages are ways to gain business or lose business**

MY WISH FOR YOU

I have a wish and an assignment for you, dear reader.

Powerful communication doesn't happen overnight. But it can grow exponentially. Even a focused process like I-A-P™ puts the onus on you to use the formula, flaunt your progress, and internalize those results. Practice, practice, practice. Keep your presentation journal updated.

My wish for you is that any anxiety you have about communicating well turns to excitement about the possibilities that accompany powerful communication. I wish you joy and success with intentional days and many WOW!'s ahead.

HELPFUL CONNECTIONS

I invite you to connect with me and *Communicate That!* to keep your powerful communication goals moving forward. Look for regular tips in multiple locations to help you *present your best.*

Roshini Multi Media	www.roshinimedia.com
Roshini's Blog	www.roshinimedia.com/blog
Twitter	www.twitter.com/RoshiniR
Communicate That!	www.communicatethatbook.com
Facebook	www.facebook.com/Roshini.Rajkumar
Roshini's E-mail	roshini@roshinimedia.com
Roshini Multi Media Phone	612.910.0826 in the United States

APPENDIX A I-A-P™ FORMULA WORKSHEET

I = Intent

A = Audience Analysis

Before the Show

During the Performance

After the Curtain Call

P = Powerful Performance

APPENDIX B
VOCAL BEHAVIOR EVALUATION

TONE

Are you enthusiastic?

Are you energetic?

Are you condescending?

Do you project confidence?

SOUND

How loud are you?

Are you nasal?

Do you have a child's voice in an adult's body?

Do you enunciate your words?

SUBTEXT

Are you aware of the messages you are sending beyond the words you speak?

What do you want to project without words?

Will your listener walk away viewing you as an authority on your subject matter?

ABOUT THE AUTHOR

Roshini Rajkumar started public speaking when she was twelve. By seventeen, she planned to become a trial lawyer but made the decision to pursue TV news days before graduating from Boston College—much to the chagrin of her South Asian mother. In between her teenage speaking roots and starting her actual career in television, she went to law school. She keeps her license current but only finds herself in a courtroom when reviewing clients' presentation styles. During her television career, Roshini reported on news and sports events, anchored the news, launched an investigative unit, and hosted talk shows on TV and radio. While part of the on-air team at WCCO (CBS) Radio Minneapolis, she won an Edward R. Murrow award for breaking news team coverage of the 2008 Republican National Convention Riot.

Roshini started Roshini Multi Media in 2006. As a keynote speaker and communication consultant, she helps people *present their best.* Her clients include businesspeople, authors, and athletes who want to WOW! within their industries or for the media. She began teaching the I-A-P™ Formula to clients not long after starting her business and is thrilled to share it with readers all over the world.

Roshini is also a commercial actor, voice talent, radio host, and contributing expert on powerful communication to local and national media. She is a guest professor at St. Catherine University's Leadership Institute. Roshini is based in Minneapolis, Minnesota, where her mother has accepted the fact her daughter doesn't practice law.